POISE
A Warrior's Guide

Gary Stokes

ISBN: 0615534732
ISBN-13: 9780615534732

Library of Congress Control Number: 2011940380
Warrior Publishers, Prescott, AZ

Contents

WARRIORS AND POISE

This is a book about getting the most out of every moment of our lives. Most of us know what it's like to get the most out of a moment, and we'd like to figure out how to do it all of the time. *Poise: A Warrior's Guide* reveals what traps us in an ordinary life and charts the path toward sustaining a fully alive state. This fully alive state is the state of poise.

We may believe that the best we can do is to enjoy life some of the time and suffer through life the rest of the time. The premise of this book is that we can increase dramatically the time we spend in joy. There is no limit to how far we can go. We can become poised all day, every day for the rest of our lives, embracing life no matter what it brings.

A significant number of the human population is pursuing good explanations about life's possibilities. These men and women are only a minority of the earth's current population, but they have enormous influence because they are the most rigorous seekers of awareness on the planet. From all walks of life and from every corner of the globe, they are systematically seeking to become more poised in order to welcome all things life brings to them each day. These seekers are creating new knowledge and new awareness for themselves and others. They work on loving others, and they work to protect our mother earth. In a human species that is still often unspeakably violent and erratic, these poised men and women make it possible for us not only to survive as a species but also to thrive and continue to emerge.

This book refers to these poised men and women as "warriors" or sometimes "warrior travelers," terms picked up from Carlos Castaneda's magisterial work about his apprenticeship to Don Juan, a warrior of stupendous poise. Warriors, or warrior travelers, are people who pursue breakthroughs in personal awareness. They are impeccable men and women who give their best at all times. In a deeper sense of impeccability, they are exquisitely aware that we are all going to die, and thus they bring a vibrant appreciation and value to every moment. Even though they are not at all morbid but, in fact, indifferent to death, warriors are keenly aware of the short time we have on earth. Knowing they have no time to waste, they come alive now, joyful, unencumbered, humble and alert.

By traversing a path of love and avoiding the worn ruts of ordinary human behavior, warrior travelers seek power, a mobilization of personal energy that allows them to witness the full wonder of the world. Because they strive to become the epitome of poise, nothing could be more fortunate than being a warrior traveler.

1

Poise: The Best Explanation

The student's goal is Poise!
Florence Shinn, *The Game of Life
and How to Play It*

Poise is a sublime state, sublime because life is at its best when we are self-possessed, self-controlled, assured, in a state of equanimity. Fully poised, we are awake, composed and balanced, free from ego, affectation, fear and embarrassment, our full powers available and ready.

Poise is the student's goal, because poise is our highest state of consciousness.

Poise gives us both pleasure and practical advantage. Poised, we are fully present in our environment, glad to be alive. Poised, we see that this moment is all we need to be happy. Balanced and composed, we are able to draw all that is pleasurable from any situation. Poised, our gratitude is complete, and our hearts are light, no matter what is happening. Poised, we enjoy the pleasure of being in love – with other people, with our mother earth, and with our own individual lives.

Poised, we live in possibility and delight. Poise is the ultimate cool, attractive and sane.

Poise brings practical advantages to every situation because—poised—we are better able to create the outcomes we want. We are able to draw on our considerable personal resources – physical, emotional, intellectual, and spiritual – to capture the full potential of the moment. Poised, we can solve problems better than we can in any other state of consciousness. We hear at our most intuitive level, see with our greatest clarity and use all our senses at their optimal level, so that we are ready to shape the life we want to create.

Only in poise do we have full access to our love. As we become more poised, we stop slipping into default and become our true selves. Thus, having clarity about the nature of poise, the thinking and behaviors that dislodge it, and the strategies for sustaining it are of utmost importance to us.

We admire poised people and observe that their obvious inner strength is an advantage in every situation. We may not always feel poised ourselves, but we want to avoid the judgments of others that inevitably come when we lose our poise. We want the approval of others, and we know that we are more attractive when we are poised. Our status among our fellows will be reduced if we are out of control, upset and off balance. So, even if we are not actually in a state of poise, we may pretend that we are, marshaling our intent to appear composed. Thus, we disguise our inner turmoil in order to gain a favored place in the social mix. Poise, in this super-ficial disguise, is, of course, a facade of social grace rather than the real thing.

But, happily, most of us achieve periods of genuine poise, and poise may be the predominant state for some of us. We are probably more poised than we used to be. Our emotional state is steadier than it used to be when confronted with chal-lenges that have now become familiar. We have learned how to absorb certain disappointments with more grace. What used to be disappointment is now simply reality.

Our loved ones have given us advice (and maybe ultimatums) about our worst indulgences—our complaining, negativ-ity, and anger. Wise counselors, therapists, and healers have given us perspective about our unresolved issues and have coached us through developmental processes that sharpened and expanded our self-awareness, helped us quiet our minds, or reduced our vulnerabilities. Superiors and colleagues at work have shined their light into our dark corners to make us aware of unproductive patterns of thinking and behavior. We may have committed to a specific spiritual practice. We have read self-help books, meditated and prayed, practiced yoga, sweated through rigorous physical regimens, listened to soothing music, smelled new aromas, played gongs and bells, and taken a hundred other developmental paths in or-der to gain serenity and peace of mind – sweet poise.

We have mellowed quite a bit, proving that our efforts have paid off. These gains are real gains, and whatever poise we have won through conscientious, intentional work we get to keep.

POISE IS THE BEST EXPLANATION
The rewards of poise are profound, as Jesus taught in the New Testament:

> The kingdom of God is in the midst of you.
> Luke 17:21

That heaven is the natural state of things and that heaven is accessible to us in this moment is a radical notion for humans convinced that life is hard, that difficulties are more common than bliss, that rapture can be achieved only after death – and even then for only the righteous.

Jesus was teaching this truth to a human race camped outside heaven's gates, even though there are no gates, there are no external barriers to entrance, and there is no password. Jesus was reporting from a completely poised consciousness that allowed him to see that everything we need for bliss is here, now, on this earth, fully available to us. Thus, to live in heaven, the student's goal must be poise.

It turns out that to be poised is to be in heaven, so let us look deeper into what is going on in a state of poise. When we understand the underlying elements of this most desirable state of consciousness, we are able to identify aspects of our current consciousness that can be strengthened. These elements are our guideposts as we expand our poise.

This book presents an explanation of life that invites us to harvest all of life's gifts. It is an explanation that refuses to call life hard names. It instead embraces everybody and everything that flows into each moment of our existence. It is an explanation that insists that we not postpone our full participation in life. This explanation is logical, coherent, and founded in fact. It invites us to acquiesce to the magisterial and unfathomable powers that guide us when we are poised.

This explanation of the poised life also deconstructs much of what we have been socialized to accept. You, I am certain, have already unlearned a great deal of what you were originally taught by your parents, teachers, and society. In this book, I use the phrase "bad explanations" to describe conventional belief and wisdom that cannot be supported in a quest for the full life. We have to understand all of the bad explanations imprinted in us by our fellow humans and make a radical shift of consciousness away from fantasy thinking, ego perspectives, rationalizations, neuroses, power positions and clichés – all part of bad life explanations. As we make the shift, life will automatically expand toward poise.

When we are poised, we are operating out of the best explanation of life. The best explanation of the full life will make clear the terrible price we pay when we lose poise, even temporarily. It will illuminate the primary cause for lost poise, so that we will be able to recognize and derail it when challenges present themselves.

Finally, this best explanation will chart the path toward sustained poise. But, first, what is the best explanation? What is poise and why is it the seeker's goal?

POISED, WE ARE PRESENT

When we are poised, we live in the now, the present moment. Serene, balanced and composed, we are not lured by the disturbed mind's rehashing of the past or its worried rehearsals of the future. Poised in this moment, we know that no moment is better than this moment. We can live our life in the now, as Eckhardt Tolle has so brilliantly explained, once we realize there is nothing except the now:

> Don't let a mad world tell you that success is anything other than a successful present moment. And what is that? There is a sense of quality in what you do, even the simplest action. Quality implies care and attention, which come with awareness. Quality requires your Presence.
>
> Eckhardt Tolle, *A New Earth: Awakening to Your Life's Purpose*

But our minds are often convinced that some other moment would be better than this moment, some other set of circumstances, some other location, some other people to be around, some other level of well-being, some other time. Our minds are convinced that there are good and bad times and that the differences are obvious.

Poised, however, the seeker is not reflexively saying no to large chunks of life.

> The Master doesn't seek fulfillment.
> Not seeking, not expecting,
> She is present, and can welcome all things.
> Lao Tzu, "The Ancient Masters"

The ancient masters of awareness Lao Tzu is describing here, masters of poise, are present, embracing life as it flows in.

We recognize and cherish the capacity of small children to live in the present, full of delight, engaging with life without inhibition or judgment. Nevertheless, we teach them a cognitive system that urges the necessity of roiling over the past and fretting about the future because we are convinced that survival requires that kind of mind. Like everyone else, the master of poise has been imprinted from birth in a cognitive system – taught to see, interpret and respond to life in a certain way.

Our cognitive system is an incredible human accomplishment designed, sustained, and improved by all of us, all of the time, to keep us safe and thriving. This brilliant, ever-unfolding creation, endlessly complicated and nuanced and, ultimately, inexplicable, is a luxurious fortress with no windows. Its inhabitants live convinced that no other worlds exist outside the world our minds understand since it contains everything known to man, including even the idea of God.

At the center of the human system of cognition is the ego, preoccupied always with its demands for recognition and attention to its injuries, busily rejecting any part of life that fails to align with its small agenda. In contrast, the master of poise – present to larger possibilities – is ready to leave the safety, the preoccupations, and communal agreements of the fort to explore the frontier, ready to move beyond the world of conventional human assumptions. Poised, the Master is present, looking, looking, breathlessly. Poised and present, we are able to say yes to the vast mystery of life.

POISED, WE ARE CONNECTED
When we are fully poised, we feel connected to all things in this marvelous universe.

Poised, the seeker treads a path of love, rejecting nothing because she sees that rejection means disconnecting, and disconnecting is abandoning the flow of life. Physicists have substantiated that everything in the universe is connected. When we fail to see that we are individually connected to everyone and everything, we do not have access to our love. Separation has a dear price:

> All disease, all unhappiness, come from the violation of the law of love. Man's boomerangs of hate, resentment, and criticism come back laden with sickness and sorrow.
> Florence Shinn, *The Game of Life and How to Play It*

Because she is poised, the seeker is not unnecessarily building and maintaining walls between herself and the people around her. Poised, she sees that we humans are all the same, ephemeral creatures who will die – the energetic fact that reduces all other differences to insignificance. Poised, we are able to love others as ourselves. Poised, we are able to forgive and able to avoid judgment. Like the great spirit Gandhi, we strive to put all mankind in our love's embrace.

Poised, we also feel connected to this beautiful earth and all its creatures. In a state of poise, we are not horrified by other life forms, never killing without provocation or necessity, never screeching like a child at a spider, a mouse, a snake or any other life form. Poised, we have the great advantage of discovery, enjoyment and learning. Poised and connected, we are committed stewards of the earth, careful, treading lightly, in harmony with all about us, like Thoreau, finding a friend in every quivering leaf. Connected to the natural world, the poised traveler through life is tapped into an endless supply of joy.

At the deepest level of poise, we also are connected to ourselves and able to intuit our life purpose. Without poise, we are unable to discern our direction, our service, our art. We are too troubled to hear. We are too much the victim to accept our assignment in love.

Poised, however, part of all we see, we are able to discern patterns and themes. We are able to notice that certain challenges present themselves to us over and over, highlighting areas of needed focus, work, and learning. Poised, we are less likely to dismiss the inner voices that call us to our potential – especially when we are called to unexpected assignments and difficult paths. At this level of connectedness, all of our powers are accessible. All of our senses are on alert. Poised, the warrior traveler sniffs out life's endless variety. Poised and connected, the warrior says yes to all of life.

POISED, WE ARE GRATEFUL

When a warrior is poised, his cup is filled to the brim, and anything you give him is more than he can take, Castaneda's mentor, Don Juan, tells us.

The masters of poise have reported that whatever life brings them is sufficient for bliss – a cup of tea, the song of a bird, a loved one's touch, the desert's bouquet when it rains, a breath of air.

We are not poised when we feel lack, when we feel that we don't have enough, when we are disappointed with what we have in this moment. Ungrateful, we are not present or connected. Lack of gratitude is devastating in its negative impacts on our lives, combining with self-absorption and self-pity to create a toxic arrogance, the antithesis of gratitude.

Gratitude, no matter what our current state of affairs, produces more abundance, in that it allows us to keep open the door for delivery of everything we have needed. As Florence Shinn says with her lighthearted faith:

> There is lavish supply, divinely planned for
> each individual. The rich man is tapping it,
> for rich thoughts produce rich surroundings.
> Florence Shinn, *The Secret Door to
> Success*

This advice is not merely wealth theology but awareness that ungrateful thinking will produce one set of life outcomes and "rich" thinking – which must be built on gratitude – will allow the delivery of "lavish supply." Here is Emerson on the same point:

> I compared notes with one of my friends who
> expects everything from the universe and is
> disappointed when anything is less than the
> best, and I found that I begin at the other ex-
> treme, expecting nothing, and am always full
> of thanks for moderate goods.... If we will
> take the good we find, asking no questions,
> we shall have heaping measures.
> Ralph Waldo Emerson, "Experience"

Gratitude is both cause and effect as we gain sublime poise. Bringing gratitude into any moment, we are more likely to be composed, humble, and alert. Grateful, we are not busy rejecting, weighing if this is a good moment or a bad moment, so we are in a state of equanimity.

Grateful in the now, we are likely to be present and connected. We energize a virtuous cycle: poised, we are able to harvest the gifts of life, which, in turn, feed our gratitude.

The more gratitude, the more poise; the more poise, the more gratitude.

Poised and grateful, we say yes to life.

POISED, WE ARE CREATIVE

Poised, we have access to our creativity. Poise may seem like a passive state—quiet and calm, best achieved alone in a state of reflection, in moments of relative inactivity.

Poise, however, is possible in all of life's moments, even in times of great physical or mental activity. We are creative creatures, changing, evolving, shaping our lives and shaping the world around us. We are artists who do their best work in a state of poise. Poise is a dynamic state because we have all our powers available.

The cosmologist Brian Swimme tells us that everything in the universe is emerging and that the universe provides all the energy required for what wants to emerge in any particular moment.

In the creative flow of what wants to emerge, we are able to harness abundant energy. We are conscious agents of the universe, creative partners in releasing what wants to emerge in ourselves and in the world around us. But only in a state of poise. Outside the boundaries of poise, our minds in service to our egos, we force our will. As Swimme points out, anything blocking what wants to emerge in the universe is destroyed.

Outside the boundaries of poise, we resist emergence. In anger, resentment, frustration, or bitterness, we are unable to discern a vision – that which might be created next. In our angst, we may be cynical that anything at all is emerging, and we are partially right at those times: nothing is emerging in ourselves because we have lost the flow, blocking the energy that could carry us into the most creative possibilities. Not able to see what wants to emerge and not engaging creatively in the moment, we put ourselves in jeopardy.

Poised, however, we are able to discern what wants to emerge. Present, connected and grateful, we offer no resistance. This is not fatalism but consciousness. Poised, we intuit our creative assignment in any moment, take advantage of the energy provided by the universe, and engage as full participants, joyful and effective.

Each of us is potentially an artist who will discover his or her full creativity in a state of poise, all of our powers at our disposal. But if we subscribe to the romantic notion that the artist is necessarily neurotic, disturbed, driven, or narcissistic, and that these forms of unhappiness are requirements for brilliant creativity, we will believe that poise is the enemy of the artist's achievement. Disturbed emotional states can produce arrestingly provocative and unique creations, but those creations may reflect the artist's distorted life, at least to some extent. The most valuable art flows from the most expansive consciousness. Poised and creative, we say yes to life.

POISED, WE ARE LIGHTHEARTED

An ancient master of awareness taught that there is a shortcut to enlightenment – that we can skip all the rigors of spiritual practice over a long period of time. The shortcut to enlightenment is simple, he said: rise in the morning from bed, go to your window and throw it open, stick your head outside, and laugh. The master knew that anyone capable of laughing at will is in a state of poise at all times. Laughing, I cannot be angry, upset, worried, or distracted.

The Egyptians believed that an afterlife in heaven was possible only if a person was lighthearted at death. Pharaohs like King Tut were buried with papyrus scrolls depicting the judge weighing the Pharaoh's heart on a scale. On the other side of the scale was a feather. A heavy heart at the end of life meant an eternity in hell. It also suggests a life spent in a cloudy consciousness.

Poised, we can detach our consciousness from the stolid earnestness of our daily concerns and laugh at ourselves, our inevitable pettiness, patterned responses, our predictable foibles. Earnestness means that we are not seeing much beyond our own thin-skinned positions. Instead, lighthearted, we are free of regret, having won this state of peace with the hard work of introspection and behavior change. Whatever harm we have done has been forgiven or corrected because we have used our suffering to learn.

We realize that our suffering is our potential calling to us, urging attention on our bad explanations. We develop better explanations and no longer repeat the negative thinking and behavior that weighed down our spirits. We are not obsessed about anything. We have no unfinished business; we are ready to sum up. Lighthearted, our love can flow. Laughter and delight are the natural response to life when we are poised.

Of course, we are not laughing in the presence of suffering of others. But even here, poised and lighthearted, our spirits have a healing effect. It does not serve the suffering to be assisted by someone also lost in suffering. Lighthearted, we are not suffering and can offer compassion and clarity. Poised and lighthearted, our love can flow.

ALL OF THE ELEMENTS OF POISE IN PLACE, WE ARE IMPERVIOUS

To say that poise means we are impervious risks the suggestion that we are walled off from injury of all sorts, like Superman or a god. We think of harm originating in external threat. Something in our environment – usually a person or persons – can do something to us that damages us, causing us discomfort, pain, or even death. These outside threats to our well-being cannot always be dodged or prevented, so when they actually materialize, we may feel violated, reduced, injured. But when we are poised, we cannot be harmed.

For harm to find me, I must believe that outside forces can alter my state of consciousness. But in a state of perfect poise, consciousness is impervious to outside forces.

> When you can no longer be disturbed, all dis-
> turbance will disappear from the external . . .
> The occult law of indifference means that
> you are undisturbed by adverse appearances.
> You hold steadily to the *constructive thought,*
> *which wins out.*
>> Florence Shinn, *The Secret Door to*
>> *Success*

Conscious people may take calculated risks, but they do not go looking for something that might damage them. We are fragile creatures: the great forces around us can destroy our bodies easily, and our egos can be as easily injured as our bodies, especially when other people prick our self-importance. So even though we are careful to avoid assaults from outside, without poise we are ever in a state of vulnerability.

The great teacher, Krishnamurti, once told an audience that the secret to his life was, "I don't mind what happens." Most people would find this a preposterous and unreasonable attitude, irresponsible and maddeningly passive. But Krishnamurti was speaking from a state of poise. Poised, he could accept whatever life brought to him and make the creative most of it. Poised, he did not spend energy on quarreling with the realities of his life or wishing that something else was appearing. Krishnamurti was impervious.

People often feel that somebody is doing something to them: "You know how to push my buttons!" But the master of poise has no buttons to push. Nobody is doing anything to anybody, let alone to a warrior, Don Juan tells Carlos Castaneda.

The poised warrior has no buttons to push, no ego to prick, no self- importance to deconstruct. The poised warrior has already deconstructed her self-importance, as this book will later illustrate, thus erasing all the buttons that made her vulnerable in the past.

To become impervious, to develop perfect poise, the warrior must see that all she has are her challenges and her decisions. There are no bad guys, there are no bad life events, and there is nothing to reject. Poised, we neutralize difficulties by framing them as challenges, and we create our lives with the decisions we make.

OUR LEARNING AGENDA

In our current consciousness, however, we come up short of perfect poise, humbled over and over by our inability to avoid negative patterns of thinking and behavior. As the stories in this book illustrate, we are often defeated by our minds, which – in service to our never-satisfied egos – resist moving into a state of humility and alertness. So, we may feel that sustaining poise is finally elusive, outside our human grasp, dooming us to face the vicissitudes of life with insufficient knowledge and awareness no matter what learning path we traverse.

Given the obvious advantages of sustaining poise, why is it so difficult for us to abandon habits of mind and behavior that clearly lead us away from living a fully vibrant and extraordinary life? Why do we find ourselves, after years of searching, learning and struggling, so out of balance at times? Still feeling angry or disappointed? Still losing our composure over trivial matters? Still blaming and judging?

Still dependent on things turning out the way we want and still circling back to despondence? How is that we are still moving through endless cycles of disappointment and defeat and then joy and victory? Why is sustained poise so elusive?

This book explores one of the final learning agendas for the warrior traveler seeking sustained poise. It is helpful to know about some barriers that typically block our path at this stage:

- The very poise that we have gained through the efforts mentioned above may now be a handicap, blocking our final thrust. We have gained poise over time, so we are happier than we used to be. Our lives may have become quite full and successful in ordinary terms. Our lapses in poise are less frequent, so even though these familiar setbacks are disturbing and troubling, we forget about them until they come around in their predictable cycle. Or, yes, something seems incomplete or something seems wrong – something like a chronic low-level virus that does not derail our life but infects our relationships and reduces our energy. Something prevents us from feeling vibrantly alive. We don't know what it is but suppose that this may be as good as it gets, so we don't have much of a personal growth agenda these days.

- Those close to us may think that we are doing well in life, with no obvious reason to take on a challenging personal transformation. No one close to us challenges us with much clarity, energy or commitment when we lose our poise. We have become predictable to them;

they have learned to accommodate the dark spaces in our awareness and the challenges of living around our flawed equilibrium. They may have attempted to address our periodic lapses in poise in the past but have given up now, driven back by our resistance to feedback and our reluctance to do the painful introspection required for learning breakthroughs. We may not have the learning partner we need right now—a person who sees potential in us and wants to go after that potential.

- The learning ahead requires the heart of a lion. Great courage is required to question patterns of thinking and behavior that keep us locked in a bubble of self-perception, trapped in an eddy, going round and round even though we have a sense that we are going somewhere. It is painful to observe how predictable we have become in certain circumstances and how well defended we are – exactly where we should offer no defense, as the examples in this book will illustrate.

Nevertheless, other seekers have gone before us, recognizing their own human frailty but listening to some call to move out onto the wild frontier where little is predictable or familiar. These intrepid warrior travelers have deconstructed the commonplace and limiting tactics of daily survival to discover rich strategies that open up new worlds. Present, connected, grateful, creative and lighthearted, they have mapped the territory.

Welcome to the frontier.

2

The Cost of Losing Our Poise

> When you lose touch with inner stillness,
> you lose touch with yourself. When you lose
> touch with yourself, you lose yourself in the
> world.
>
> Eckhart Tolle, *Stillness Speaks*

Often we lose our poise, not over significant challenges, but over small provocations in the most mundane circumstances. Mary, a warrior traveler and my wife, laughs with me now about this incident of lost poise, but she didn't find it humorous when it happened and neither did I. Here Mary tells The Bubble Wrap Story, as it has come to be known at our house:

> I went to the garage to retrieve some bubble wrap I had stored in the storage cabinet to use for packing a gift I was about to ship. I couldn't find it and went back into the house,

hollering, "Gary, have you seen the bubble wrap? I said where is the bubble wrap that was in the garage?"

"I used it to pack something I shipped," Gary said.

Angry now and in my strictest voice of admonishment, "I wish you would consider someone else for a change before you use something of theirs."

Gary, stopping work, alert to trouble, "That bubble wrap had been in the garage for three years. I needed it for a business shipment and used it."

Irritated even more by this defense, I said, "I have been saving that bubble wrap so I would have it when I need it, and now it isn't there. I just wish you could think about other people and check with me before you use something of mine."

As usual, Gary tried to get me to lighten up by pointing out the absurdity of the situation: "I see now that I should have asked you at the time, 'Say, lover, do I have your permission to use the bubble wrap that's been taking up space in the garage for three years?'"

> Standing now in his office doorway, hands on hips like a cartoon wife, I say, "It's hopeless to try to get any consideration out of you. Next time I want to use something of yours, I won't bother to ask, believe me!"

> I would remain frustrated and disgruntled toward Gary for several hours. I lost my poise and found it difficult to find my way back.

Well, we could say in retrospect, this is the stuff of television sitcoms – a humorous and harmless example of what perfectly nice people do all the time. But in real life, our incidents of lost poise are not harmless. We suffer when we lose our poise, and the people around us probably suffer when we lose our poise.

Unexamined, whatever stresses trigger our distraught emotions and then fuel conflicts will surely come around again and again. These incidents of lost poise are rarely one-time occurrences but are part of predictable patterns that keep us anchored in a murky state of consciousness and a set of bad explanations about how we're relating to life.

Mary is a wonderfully poised person most of the time, but she has noticed that she slides into a default mode of anger and victimhood when certain things don't go her way. Here is her analysis of what the bubble wrap incident felt like to her and what the incident cost her:

> Looking back at this incident is humbling, because I hate to think that such a

non-consequential problem could shatter my poise. I was addicted to the idea of right and wrong. Feeling wronged by Gary, I granted him power over my emotional life. I want to get to the bottom of this dynamic and break the pattern that I've been in for some time – maybe my entire life: the pattern of not taking full responsibility for my inner state.

Every element of poise discussed in Chapter One fell apart when I found out that Gary had used my entire bubble wrap inventory.

- Presence: I was hardly the Master that Lao Tzu describes; I was not present, and I was certainly not welcoming all things. Even though I know that every moment of life is precious, I angrily rejected what life was presenting to me in that moment.

- Connectedness: Going unconscious, I lost my connection with Gary, the man I love, my friend, trusted ally, lover and fellow warrior traveler. I talked to him as if he were the enemy, a dumb and careless one at that. Poise gone, I felt separate and created a harmful disconnect between us. I really wasn't connected to anything outside my own wants and expectations. For the moment, I was a narcissist.

- Gratitude: I obviously wasn't feeling any gratitude. I was unconscious of my incredible blessings. Most of the time I realize with great gratitude that we have achieved the American Dream and much more, yet in this moment I was lost in my ego's sense of entitlement and couldn't appreciate anything about my fortunate life.

- Creativity: Angry and self-absorbed, I acted like I had no options, even though they were numerous. I could have invented some alternative packaging solution from other materials around the house. I could have packed up my box and added bubble wrap later, after I purchased some more. I could have practiced my poise by asking Gary if he had finally gotten rid of the bubble wrap that took up so much space in the storage cabinet all these years. Maybe the best one would have brought Gary and me even closer than we are normally. I could have come to him affectionately with a joke about the bubble wrap: had he been popping bubbles behind my back? I could have turned what at first looked like a problem for me into something that enhanced my life. I know that we can do that with any challenge, but it wasn't obvious in the moment when creativity was needed.

- Lightheartedness: Needless to say, I went temporarily insane and was unable to laugh at myself. How could I lose perspective so completely? I need to remember the importance of not being earnest. I've told my women's group this story, and now they all introduce their own stories about lost poise with, "I had a bubble wrap moment...," and we all laugh hilariously over our occasional craziness, so something good has come of my preposterous behavior. I'm laughing late, but I'm laughing.

LOSS OF POISE SEEMS NORMAL

We underestimate how much a lack of poise limits our lives, even though we know that, outside the boundaries of poise, life is much less enjoyable, less predictable, and less safe. When our poise is dislodged, we make mistakes, misinterpreting what's going on around us, responding to our environment inappropriately, and creating even more challenges and confusion.

People who lose their poise completely may seem emotionally unhinged to us, and we feel crazy ourselves when our shattered poise leaves us thinking and doing things that produce negative results in our life. Trying to regain our composure later, we may feel guilt and regret, wondering why we seem to repeat these cycles of behavior that leave us remorseful, hapless and defeated. Without poise, good mental health is impossible to achieve and sustain, as the stories in this chapter illustrate.

As a species, humans normalize being out of balance, upset and reactionary. In some arenas, anger and rejection of life have become the norm, acceptable behavior. To be poised in certain situations is interpreted as unresponsive, inappropriate, disloyal, cold, or uncaring. Cultural support for victimhood is endemic. Angry, aggressive, even violent responses to the life around us have been accepted and encouraged by people throughout human history. And though many people may disapprove of such responses, we seem locked into a mindset that defends those responses as normal and necessary when we believe that our well-being is at risk.

When very conscious people decide to respond to injustice peacefully, as leaders of the U.S. civil rights movement did, for instance, they test the limits of our individual and communal poise. When a new poised strategy like passive resistance is politically successful and higher levels of justice are achieved, we have evolved as a species, even though many in society remain trapped in victimhood, angry and resentful, unable to participate in our human victory.

We find it relatively easy to justify ourselves when we lose our poise. Our bodies signal threats to our brains, whether the perceived threats can actually harm us or not, and we defend ourselves, often losing our poise in the process. Making it easier to rationalize our fearful and reflexive behaviors, society legitimizes a broad range of emotional responses to life's challenges – including expressions of anger, frustration, impatience, and other responses that destroy our poise. With society's tacit approval, we may develop clichéd responses to life – life is hard, life is not fair, life sucks – partly in humor and partly to defend the legitimacy of our self-pity and our aggressive behavior.

This book questions the legitimacy of these negative emotions – not their value and reality as visceral reactions to whatever is going on in the moment – but as default bases for any decision in the moment.

All a warrior has are his challenges and his decisions, teaches Don Juan to Castaneda. Decisions made in unconscious response to powerful emotions are made outside the clarity of poise and thus suffer from distortion. Even when our unconscious behavior results in disaster, we may still argue that our reactions were right – believing more in our emotions than in conscious, considered, and deliberate decision-making. In other words, our egos out of control, hurt, and continuing to suffer, we defend chaos over poise.

The worst error we make when we lose our poise is to say no to life. Our anger, frustration and impatience, for instance, are a rejection of what is happening. We reject what materializes in the moment. If we fail to bring this rejection to consciousness in the next moment, we will necessarily lose our poise.

This chapter gives examples of people losing their poise and exposes the great cost to us when we do. The most extreme examples of lost poise are not examined here: the murderous acting out of angry people throughout history; the incredible cruelties people perpetrate on others when they lose their balance completely and become brutal instruments of their fear, hatred, and need for dominance and power; the mass destruction caused by entire societies gone mad.

Instead, the examples here are reported or observed experiences of introspective adults, who, by and large, are leading decent, peaceful lives. Usually, the people losing their poise in these examples want to be balanced, happy, generous, and sane. They abhor losing their self-control. Even though they may lose their poise in predictable patterns, most of them would welcome deeper self-understanding that would allow them to stay poised even when significant challenges present themselves with their families, co-workers, neighbors, and fellow citizens.

COST NO. 1: WE SUFFER AND LOSE OUR ABILITY TO ENJOY LIFE

When we lose our poise, we feel like a leaf at the mercy of the wind, out of control, blown this way and that by the forces around us. We are not directing our reactions to the challenges of our life, with the result that we lose confidence. Stumbling and confused, we experience some degree of helplessness. Suffering fills our psychic space and we find it difficult to work our way back to poise. We may be stuck in self-pity for long periods, identifying other people as the culprits. Our poise gone for the time being, we cannot laugh at ourselves and cannot enjoy our lives.

This book argues that we should and can sustain poise even in the most challenging situations. The following example of how we suffer and lose our ability to enjoy life when we lose our poise is chosen because we may think that we cannot – or even should not – maintain our poise under certain circumstances. We may feel strongly that a great injustice has been done to us, for instance, warranting our anger and blown poise.

As the story below illustrates, however, losing our poise is always a self-created set of thinking and behaviors that sabotage our capacity to say yes to life, no matter what is happening. Losing our poise inevitably reduces or eliminates our ability to enjoy life.

1,000 ARROWS

Two professional acquaintances of mine lost their poise when they were fired from a lucrative training contract with a respected organization. They had been hired as a consulting team to coach the organization's managers, but ran into disagreement with the organization's CEO over their approach midway through the contract. When they were unwilling to align with the CEO's perspective, insisting that their approach was correct, their contract was terminated.

Even though they advertised themselves as spiritual masters and teachers of human consciousness, they were unable to maintain their poise. Angry and upset, they immediately created a victim story to explain their anguish.

One member of the team said that he felt like "St. Andrew, pierced by 1,000 arrows." His partner said that she "felt like a trapped animal" and threatened legal action. As they drove away from the organization's training site, their car plunged off the road onto its side in the ditch. They were not injured, but the accident became part of the melodrama they recited to friends for months afterward about how the CEO had tyrannized them and how much they had suffered at his hands.

Stories like this one seduce us because we can easily sympathize with people who claim injustice caused by people in power, and we have empathy for people who are suffering. It's not easy to see through stories like this unless we understand that suffering is a choice, as it is here. The two consultants would argue, perhaps, that they had no choice but to suffer. How could anyone enjoy life when they are summarily dismissed, treated so rudely, their work rejected?

But these two competent, usually upbeat, cheerful people with a long career in coaching people about human relationships forgot what they claimed to know. Losing their poise, they were not able to stay present, welcoming anything that life presented in the moment, as if this moment in their lives wasn't as good as any other moment. They lived in a good-part-of-life/bad-part-of-life paradigm in which some of life measures up to expectations and some of life disappoints. In a poised paradigm, in which all life is to be honored, they could have said, "Ah, now this." Instead, they left the scene saying, "No, not this!"

They were not able to stay connected but separated themselves from the people they were working for. They had been unable to adjust to the organization's requests and were unable to maintain their connection with the CEO. They did not have to separate themselves but could have kept everyone, including the CEO, in their love's embrace. In this incident, feeling wounded, the teachers of love lost access to their own love.

They were not grateful. They were unable to see the richness of this situation – not able to be grateful for the opportunity and money they had earned and not able to be grateful for the learning opportunity presented by their termination. They pretended as if they had played no part in what happened to them and could only feel deprived and cheated – thus the threat of legal action.

Their creativity was absent, and they simply moved into the ordinary default perspective of complaint and self-pity. Instead of suffering, they could have decided to try some creative responses, such as asking for specific feedback about their performance that led to their termination. They could have remembered that they are creating every aspect of their lives – consciously or unconsciously – and could have speculated about why they sought this contract, what they had failed to notice about their relationship with the CEO, why they had gotten themselves fired, and why they needed to lose control and end up in the ditch – taking full responsibility for what happened. Instead, they took no responsibility and missed the lessons that this incident had to offer them.

Obviously, they were heavy-hearted, unable to do anything but invite supporters into sympathetic rescue.

Is it absurd to suppose that we can maintain a light heart in the face of adversity? No, it is not absurd; poised people are able to do it, as we will see later in the book. You, no doubt, some of the time, have been able to maintain a light heart when faced with difficult challenges, so you know that it is possible.

Had the consultants been capable of lightheartedness, they might have been able to avoid being terminated in the first place. We are in a high state of vulnerability when we require that others respect our self-importance and when we find ourselves overly earnest about the vicissitudes of life. Had the consultants been able to laugh as they drove away, they probably would not have gone into the ditch.

To lose poise is to lose control of how we are thinking and behaving. Not poised, it is impossible to enjoy life because we are rejecting some element of it. Not poised, we suffer unnecessarily.

COST NO. 2: WE LOSE PERSPECTIVE AND MAKE BAD DECISIONS

We can't make good decisions when we lose our poise. Our perspective becomes too small and too warped. Not poised, we are unable to see how we are creating a self-defeating response to the challenges before us. We have become separate, at war with someone or something. Rejecting what life has presented, resentment displaces gratitude. Just when we most need to develop options, our creativity is wasted protecting our wounded egos. Heavy and earnest, we can only stagger behind the protection of our rationalizations.

When we are poised, all of our powers are turned on. We will make the best judgments possible when we are poised and can step back at peace once our decisions are made. Poised, we are humble and alert, opening ourselves to the broadest perspective. As the results of our actions unfold–whatever the outcome–we know that we have given our best. This is the great advantage of the warrior traveler.

Those who lose their poise under duress, however, will not enjoy this advantage, but will inevitably suffer further as a result of their bad decisions.

I am familiar with the following example of lost poise, distorted perspective and bad judgment through newspaper coverage and court proceedings of a case in my home community. I'll use a different name of the principal actor in this melodrama to avoid providing him with further embarrassment. He has already paid a high cost for his lost poise, not the least of which was public humiliation.

ROAD RAGE

Jack Compton was 64 years old and retired when this case began. He was driving his Jaguar on a spring afternoon through the busy central business district when he came up behind a bicycle at a red light. When the light turned green, the bicycle accelerated to the speed limit, 25 mph. But Compton accelerated to within inches of the bicycle's rear tire and stayed in that threatening position as they moved down the street.

The rider of the bike reported later in court that he signaled the driver to either pass or back off, but Compton continued to follow within inches of the bike. A witness reported to police that the situation was "very dangerous" and he thought the car was about to hit the bike.

Compton told the police later that he was "frustrated and angry" that the bicycle was going slow and taking up the entire lane. Most of us have seen the agitated faces of other drivers in our rearview mirrors. Sometimes they are talking angrily to themselves. Sometimes they are making hostile gestures. We worry about what these drivers might do next because we instinctively know that they, having lost their poise, are not likely to make the best decisions.

In the case above, Compton lost all perspective in the moment and made a very bad decision. We could argue that he didn't make a decision at all but instead, "angry and frustrated," slid into default – his self-importance pricked and his ego wanting to dominate the situation.

Even after being charged with a misdemeanor, the driver failed to regain his poise, insisting on his bad explanation of what happened – as evidenced by his pleading innocent and demanding a jury trial. Incredibly, because he continued to insist on his innocence, Compton required nine separate court hearings over 15 months before he was found guilty. His distorted judgments required witnesses, lawyers, jurors, court staff and police to give enormous amounts of time and energy to his lost poise. Still, he was unable to understand his responsibility for what happened.

The jury held him accountable for his bad decision, however, and he paid the price of legal fees, fines of $1500, required traffic school, community service, probation and public embarrassment.

Notice in this story the impact of losing connection with other people. In his anger and impatience, the driver separated himself from the cyclist, and then his perceptions became distorted. He became convinced that his aggressive behavior was warranted. He is a man of mature years, retired, driving a luxury automobile, but – in the moment – he had no gratitude and no creativity. His poise blown, he failed to make good decision when his emotions arose.

When we lose our poise, lose perspective and make bad decisions, life gives us feedback. If we're open to the feedback, we can make course corrections. If we fail to heed the feedback, life has a way of increasing the intensity of the feedback, giving us chance after chance to wake up at last. In this story, Compton received an enormous amount of intense feedback over an extended period of time, but he was unable to regain perspective and unable to revise his bad decisions. He paid a high price for his lost poise.

MACRO AND MICRO PERSPECTIVES

Obviously, we cannot sustain poise and make good decisions when our perspectives are warped significantly by being too narrowly focused on ourselves. So, what is a perspective that might be large enough to be useful in framing any particular challenge that comes our way?

A useful macro perspective comes from astrophysicists who tell us that we may live in a universe, perhaps multi-verses, full of nuclear explosions, anti-matter, black holes, and spectacular new formations. In explaining quantum mechanics, physicist David Deutsch tells us that we may live in infinite universes with infinite numbers of earths and with infinite numbers of humans. In this unimaginable mystery, what is my place, my value, my job to do, if I have a job to do?

Some thinkers suppose that our job is to help the universe become aware of itself. Cosmologist Brian Swimme, with his enormous perspective, suggests that the universe wants life and wants community, thus explaining the likelihood of a life-friendly earth in a universe where life cannot emerge except under perfect conditions.

How can my challenges cause me to lose poise in these macro perspectives? The bike rider in front of my car is slowing me down? Ah.

People who see God behind these great mysteries have a macro perspective as well. Spiritual practice, then, becomes the retention of this all-encompassing perspective. Used as a frame for thinking and behaving in any particular moment, a loving God becomes the truth and reality that helps believers stay humble and alert, accessing their love and serving others. It's hard to find a reason to lose my poise if I believe that a perfect God has a perfect purpose. That biker is in my way? Ah.

But most people are unable to stay fully conscious of the macro, even if they are aware of it, and even if they find a good explanation for life within a particular macro perspective. So we swing forever back and forth between consciousness and unconsciousness, as one of the ancient masters said.

The micro perspective is in play when we lose our poise. At the extremes, we are solipsistic, thinking and acting as if we are the only thing that exists – that all existence is within us. Or, much more commonly, we are narcissistic, thinking and behaving as if we are the only interesting and valuable person in our environment. These micro perspectives give us plenty of rationale for lost poise in a childlike existence in which my needs are paramount, and anything that blocks what I want cannot be tolerated. A cyclist is slowing me down? A huge deal in the micro, where pettiness rules.

COST NO. 3: OUR POTENTIAL EVAPORATES

Our potential is the richer life that is possible for us, if we learn. Our potential is our destiny, what we must invite, move toward and develop. Our potential is the only future worthy of our attention, and it has the best chance to emerge when we're sustaining our poise.

Poised, we're present and connected, so we are able to hear what wants to emerge in our lives. We are able to see larger contexts for decisions. We are grateful and lighthearted so we are not blocking new possibilities with negative emotions and thinking. We're able to enjoy life as it flows in with all its possibilities. Our creativity is not jammed by micro perspectives. We're open, allowing our genius to explore. Poised, we're in the flow.

When we lose our poise, in contrast, our potential evaporates, at least temporarily, and it expires permanently if we don't gain clarity about our bad explanations of what is going on. When we lose our poise, what was possible is less possible now. Without access to our magnificent creativity, we cannot improvise and must slip into default. We become a smaller self.

What might be easy to solve creatively remains obscured and under-invested. Our relationships, which could help us move toward our potential, are damaged. Others are less inclined to invest in our development when we have lost our composure, have distorted reality, and have refused responsibility for our behavior. Without poise, our gifts and talents are clouded – to ourselves and to those around us.

Off balance and confused, we find it nearly impossible to learn anything significant. We refuse to accept that we are creating our life when we lose our poise, so we stop creating what we want and, instead, give away our powers to others who seem to be controlling us. Now we become predictable, locked into thinking and behavior that keeps us in the eddy, circling and circling, going nowhere.

Here's an example of how chronic lost poise shuts off potential.

A divorced woman I know loses her poise every time she crosses paths with her ex-husband and every time he comes up in conversations with her children or other family members who have a relationship with both of them. This pattern has been going on for an astounding forty years because she has never forgiven him, has never come to terms with her own bitterness and has never stopped repeating her explanation for what happened – an explanation that describes her ex as an "evil" man. Relatives who know them both disagree with her assessment but have had to accommodate her predictable anger, anguish, and bitterness. It is easy for others to see how she abandons her poise when her ex-husband comes into the picture.

At family weddings where both attend, she is unable to maintain her usual social grace and moves into default. Preoccupied with ancient wounds, she recreates them and brings them into the celebration. She can't be present, unable to focus on the couple or event being celebrated. Her anger returns, and she feels isolated when she observes other family members being friendly to him, convinced that they are disloyal to her and feeling betrayed. She is unable to create a different mood, stubbornly refusing to experiment with alternative thinking or behavior that might free her from the straitjacket of judgment. In the midst of joy, she is earnest and rigid. She has lost her poise and can't retrieve it.

Even though she has a brilliant mind that allowed her to excel in higher education, master several languages and pursue a professional career, she has not fulfilled her potential. Her pattern of heavy judgment of people she does not approve of has kept her anchored in pessimism. She is frequently ill and depressed. Years ago, people who knew her well saw great potential in what appeared to be a gifted woman of unusual intellect, physical beauty and moral clarity. She is able to maintain poise when she is not focused on the people and situations that trouble her, but those people and situations keep coming into her consciousness with painful regularity.

Our potential never stops calling to us from the unconscious, even if we ignore it for a lifetime.

It is easy for us to recognize the bad explanations that keep our loved ones rigid and barricaded. So we shine our light into our loved one's dark corners, offering better explanations, offering dialogue, offering encouragement, and challenges. This is love in action. If, over time, our love is consistently refused – in other words, if there is no receptivity but only resistance, anger, or hopelessness – we will inevitably pull back, respecting that our love is not welcome or productive.

In this example, relatives and friends have learned not to approach her with alternative views that might release her from her unhappiness. She does not allow any dialogue that explores her anguish. She is easily angered if loved ones suggest she might not be viewing life correctly. Family and friends have gently pulled their time and energy away from her. Now in her 70s, she is isolated, with no one encouraging her or challenging her anymore. Chronic lost poise has exacted a harsh price in her life. It is fair to say that, because of her refusal to learn, she has no potential.

COST NO. 4: WE DO NOT HAVE FULL ACCESS TO OUR LOVE

When we lose our poise, we lose access to our love of other people, our love of our life-nurturing planet and our love of life itself. Poise disrupted, our love becomes pinched, gasping for air, or displaced entirely by our preoccupations with whatever element of life we are rejecting.

Listening deeply, caring and responding with empathy and compassion to others requires poise. Not poised, we may be able to muster some bit of attention for someone else, but we will reserve most of our energy for our suffering ego. If we are unable and unwilling to sustain poise, we have essentially exiled ourselves from our responsibility to love others as ourselves and have resigned as stewards of the earth.

During periods when we have lost access to our love, we inevitably take more from life than we give. Poised, we know that we have everything we need. Our cups are filled to the brim, we're grateful and generous, and our love flows naturally.

Not poised, we stop giving. We stop being generous. Our love is dammed behind our self-pity. It will be apparent to those around us that we are not giving much, but we're absorbed in our victim story so we don't have much self-awareness about how pinched we have become. We feel justified in withholding our generosity because we feel wronged by somebody or something. We have narrowed our life to a sliver of what is possible. This shrunken life is the bankrupting cost of failing to sustain our poise.

Everyone in your life would like to be loved by you. Everyone you meet would like to be a beneficiary of your understanding, affection, kindness, respect, attention, and investment. You, for your part, no doubt, would like to give everyone the love they need from you, and you often do. When you are poised, your love flows generously and easily. Poised, you are able to take all people into your embrace. When you have full access to your love, you know what it is like to be outside your ego, above the vicissitudes of the moment, to be your true self.

But then we lose our poise again.

TRYING TO SUSTAIN POISE: A CASE STUDY IN ACCESSING LOVE

This story is a case study in how difficult it is to sustain poise in order to access love at a time of great stress.

With this poignant series of e-mailed self-reports over a period of months from my friend, Fran, we see how we struggle to love at times, even though our own values require it of us. Fran's need to have access to her love of her husband at all times is clear when a cancerous tumor was discovered between the cortexes of his brain. Their lives were suddenly transformed.

Fran has considerable self-awareness. She respects poise as the goal, and she notices how it is disrupted when she feels sorry for herself. She understands how she moves in and out of access to her love when she fails to remain poised. Her report illustrates how difficult it is to understand and suppress self-pity.

A few days after the initial diagnosis, Fran reported her struggle to stay poised in this email:

> So much has happened since then. Rich is doing fine, but he's very tired at the end of the day and goes to bed at 8:00. I'm doing better but the least thought of what he's going through, and my composure is gone. He spoke to me today about my distraction and lack of focus. He's right. We almost had an accident while I was driving right on our street. A driver in a big truck turned abruptly in front of me to enter his driveway. I slammed on the brakes, and we didn't col-

lide but it was too close. I think he never saw us.

Thank heaven I was quick enough to react, but Rich is right. I'm distracted, almost dreamy, have a hard time getting anything done and cry very easily. After his little talk, I realized I lapse into a helpless feminine act too often. I vent my sadness. I wonder how much of it is a childish stab at "see me," a frightened woman looking, of all places, to Rich for comfort. So, that's the first lesson. His load is much greater than mine.

The message is to stay in the day we have right now, which is very satisfactory. Troubles will come later, but they aren't here now. So that's the mode. Settle down, drive safely, get necessary jobs done. There's no margin for error these days.

Fran is battling hard to sustain her usual poise, but she cannot stay present, her worries pulling her out of the moment, "distracted, almost dreamy." She realizes that her connection to Rich is partly a need of support from him, knowing that a more poised response would be focused on his needs rather than her own. She tries to maintain gratitude, arguing with herself, "The message is to stay in the day we have right now, which is very satisfactory." But instead of gratitude, at times she feels sadness and fear.

She has not been effective but wants to bring a creative response to the situation, rallying herself to settle down and do what is necessary in an efficient way that recognizes that "there is no margin for error these days."

Finally, Fran has been unable to maintain her usual light-heartedness in the face of this crisis. Lighthearted, she could bring a steady love to her husband, capturing every precious moment with him, boosting his spirits with her lightness. Instead, her own suffering interferes with the focus, support and caring she wants to provide to her husband.

Fran reports in the next e-mail that Rich's surgery to remove the brain tumor has been scheduled:

> I'm really living a miracle right now. I've been terribly tense, jumping at Rich's every call, which isn't often but enough to induce strain – though it was more my attitude. I was operating on pure emotion, crying at the drop of a pin. The most dangerous words for me were "How are you?"
>
> Then, about a week ago, Rich woke me about 3 in the morning to say he'd been aware of my strain, which was showing in forgetful-ness and lack of focus. He assured me things were all right, and he didn't want me hurt by all of this. I was so grateful and woke up nor-mal. I'm now able to share his robust humor on this topic. It's all a bluff, of course, but

it's ok. It's a fine way to live right now so I'm quite back to normal, and he's doing very well.

BUT the main thing for me, and I feel it in my bones, is how I'm surrounded by the love of friends. I feel it like a survivor of a flood feels the rubber raft that comes floating by. You (friends) sustain me. It's palpable. I can almost touch it. It's life changing. Thank you thank you thank you.

Fran has not been able to regain much poise in the weeks since she realized that her husband might die. The elements of poise are there some of the time, but she darts from living in a miracle to tension and strain. She understands that battles are going on within herself, but her creativity is dormant, and she must be rescued by her very ill husband to recover normalcy.

She is grateful for support, using the raft metaphor to let her friends know how much she still needs their rescue, as well as her husband's. Not poised, she cannot keep her husband in the center of concern but can only see herself in the middle of this drama, "surrounded by the love of friends." Assured by her husband that "things were all right," she deftly places her own emotional needs center stage, and she remains the grateful victim, surrounded by her nurturing audience.

Following radiation treatment to remove Rich's tumor, but with his future still in doubt, Fran is aware of her uncharacteristic loss of balance and attempts to gain perspective. She reports her inability to sustain poise with great insight and candor:

> I have a goal – to walk the path I've been given with courage, truth, grace and humor. Having this challenge and having decided how to get through it has made things ever so much easier – but they're easy right now anyway because Rich is feeling good, he's highly productive, writing poetry and letters, calling people, setting to the task of saying things he's never said, settling some accounts, explaining some situations, even very old ones. It gives him an edge. He has a look on his face that indicates he's going to spring a little surprise. He's resolutely staying in charge of himself.

> My part is to clear the way so he can do all this: help him buy stamps, help him get his special stationery designed, take him to pick it up and so forth. This doesn't use much of my time even though it sounds like it might. I can't stay in a selfless manner of servitude very long. Actually it isn't necessary for very long, but I find I need to get away sometimes, hole up with a book, get out of the house and see someone else for coffee. These moments are accompanied by irritability. Little things nag at me. I use my control so probably no one would guess the present moment has irritated me.

This state of mind is outside poise. I am keenly aware of the condition of the moment. It's like going from stepping-stone to stepping-stone, each one of them being a moment of immediate awareness. I keenly sense these moments but I'm not in charge of them at all. I'm responding to them like a leaf in the wind, so far hanging on just fine.

The thread through all of this is that Rich is getting born into a man he never knew existed, and I'm a witness of the process, sometimes doing what I can to enable it. It's a rarified, magical time. Sometimes I'm tuned in. Sometimes I'm bored with it. Sometimes I'm titillated and thrilled. Sometimes I really need a break. Sometimes I'm really pissed, but the bottom line is always that my behavior, or how I'd like to behave, must not curtail Rich's moments of birth. I'm comfortable with that, even when pissed. Maybe what I'm saying is I feel like a leaf in the wind, but it is part of a very strong tree, and maybe at the heart of things, that's poise.

Yes, there is some poise there, but there also was the potential to be with Rich in a way that had no neediness attached. Had Fran been able to sustain poise, her love would not have been constantly interrupted by elements of internal drama – irritation, dreaminess, fears.

These thoughts and behaviors are born from self-pity. Each time she wrestles unsuccessfully with her conflicted emotions regarding Rich and his imminent death, she moves out of the moment and takes her love with her.

Soon after, Rich died in Fran's arms. Two weeks after his death, Fran writes about reading a pamphlet on grieving. She reports that she is feeling most of the grieving symptoms, but her love is flowing, nevertheless:

> The pamphlet refers to The Loved One. I think about Rich almost all the time.
>
> There are pictures of him in strategic places, right here at the computer and by the sink in the bathroom. His shirts hang in the closet. I bury my face in them and then go to bed. It's a way of saying good night.

Nevertheless, her ambivalence about her husband continues.

> A friend close enough to notice said once, "I'll bet Rich isn't easy to be married to." I mentioned this to another friend later, and she snorted, "Is any man?" Well, good question.

This excerpt of an e-mail illustrates clearly how it is not other people or life challenges that trigger our lost poise. It is always our self-pity raging away in our minds that insists on poisoning the precious now with long-past victim stories. After Rich's death, with two helpers, Fran peers into their old barn full of Rich's machinery and junk for the first time in years.

The thing that sent me over the edge was my 1959 Jaguar, a sleek little white sedan I bought for $2,000 about 35 years ago. I've driven it perhaps two weeks in all the time I've owned it. British-made Jaguars of that era don't do well in Southern California. They need a complete overhaul to function here. Rich was always going to get to it. For years I believed him.

Also, for years I forgot I owned a Jaguar sedan. I forgot right to the minute when I led Don and Jack to the garage, and there was my Jag, dark gray with dust, buried behind a stack of tires. My soul gasped, "Oh migawd!" I looked inside. The interior stunk of rats. Chewed pieces of the roof lining lay on the seats.

My heart broke, and I was furious with Rich. He's been gone 14 days, and I am furious with him. So much for grieving about my Loved One.

Fran resurrects her dead husband, at least briefly, and loses her poise once again. Even though she had forgotten the car, she is incensed that Rich had failed her once again. Self-pity fired up, she invents another victim story to explain her distraught feelings and to re-ignite her case that Rich had been difficult to live with.

Deeply conflicted between love and fury I went to bed. In the morning I felt better. Every part of me wanted to love Rich. I realized we'd just had a fight. I'd made up. I buried my face in his shirts. I have his belt in a roll by his picture at the sink. I touched it remembering how it wrapped around his waist.

I let go of the Jaguar, as I have in the past, making the conscious decision that loving Rich was more important, but I also went to see a counselor who has been invaluable off and on for a while. In her office, I got a better picture of what loving is. It's a commitment to the whole person.

There were parts of Rich that made me uncomfortable. If I could have picked and chosen I'd have taken his voice, his intelligence, his passion for me, his sense of humor, his love of music, his appreciation for the authentic and the real, his reliable grasp of the larger issues, his moral courage, his attention to and love of our home and my art, and discarded his lack of focus on the goals I wanted for him, his procrastination, the dirt picked up around old cars, and his gruffness when he was irritated.

… I saw that in our 38 years together, there was no doubt we loved each other. His love of me was open and uncomplicated. My love for him was stormy because that is the way I am. I want certain things and get mad if I

don't get them, but under all my storminess
was the certainty that I'd return to loving
Rich when my storm blew over.

Trying to summarize their relationship, Fran rationalizes her
anger and self-pity in the marriage. "My love for him was
stormy because that's the way I am." What was stormy were
the times, still occurring now even after there is no husband
to be stormy about, when Fran was angry, feeling sorry for
herself and losing her poise. She puts a shine on her behavior
by calling it stormy and implying that her angry reactions
aren't really a serious part of their marriage dynamic.

She is convinced that the issues of the marriage were caused
by Rich's difficult personality, habits and behavior. Instead
of taking full responsibility for the marriage she created for
herself, she justifies her lack of poise by speaking through
her friend: "I'll bet Rich isn't easy to be married to." She
does not assume that her "storminess" caused any problems
in the marriage, since she virtuously returns to loving her
husband after each storm.

All of the responsibility for marital problems is given to
Rich, the projection that marks every victim story. But it's
a bad explanation, presented with brilliant seductiveness.
Well, most people might say, what a nice woman. She had
a difficult man to live with, but she loved him much of the
time. When she wasn't angry at him.

Fran is, indeed, a good woman, but a better explanation of
her marriage might contrast Rich's open and uncomplicated

love for his wife with Fran's love, which is complicated, ambivalent and interrupted by patches of anger and
irritation.

Like most people, Fran wants to pick and choose what war-
rants her love and what doesn't. She was able to love when
Rich's qualities aligned with her own needs and predilections,
but not able when she didn't get what she wanted. After his
death, she begins to see that love embraces the entire person.

There is plenty of love here. Love flames much of the time,
then flickers and goes out, smothered by self-pity and victim
explanations. But Fran always re-ignites her love. She has an
extraordinary capacity for self-revelation. She has an eagle
eye for her own melodrama, and she has the courage to look
deeply at what she sees. She is close to a breakthrough in
poise that would allow her to move self-pity into the background and take full responsibility for the life she is creating.
Until then, without full access to her love, she will suffer
with her storminess.

Many would argue that Fran's marriage is about as good as
we can do. This is the human argument when we stop short
of our potential. This argument is not true.

STOPPING SHORT OF OUR POTENTIAL
We are used to losing our poise. Yes, we know that life cannot
be enjoyed when our poise is shattered, but we don't expect
to enjoy everything in life anyway. Yes, we know that we lose
perspective when we come unglued, but we rationalize that
everybody does it. We suspect that our potential may shrink if

we can't sustain poise, but we think the shrinkage is not significant enough to worry about. We might even notice that we
aren't very loving when we go crazy, but – well – the people
around us know that we're good people and they forgive us.

We are aware, usually in retrospect, that we have lost our
poise when we are most out of control – acting out our anger,
desperately frightened and retreating from life's challenges
or abandoning our principles and values in some obvious
way. Much of the time, though, we don't even notice that
we have lost our poise. We have normalized our irritation
over minor challenges, our many ways of feeling unhappy
or distracted or self-absorbed, our habitual petty arguments
with life.

We don't feel entirely alone when we can't sustain poise
because society provides plenty of support when we act
outside poise, an unfortunate reality discussed in detail in
the next chapter. We may have come to the untenable position that it is not desirable to be poised all of the time, even
arguing that our lack of poise is a virtue – our lack of equanimity and our emotional eruptions proof that we are fully
engaged in life, our suffering somehow proof that we are
sensitive human beings. These rationalizations may help us
feel linked with an ever-troubled human race, but they also
make significant learning about ourselves impossible.

The next chapter reveals how we lock ourselves away from
our potential.

3

How We Lose Our Poise

> I consider the basic personality in our time is
> a neurotic personality.
> Fritz Perls, *Gestalt Therapy Verbatim*

A universal pattern unfolds when we lose our poise, a pattern of emotional response, thinking and behavior that, in a moment, exiles presence, connectedness, gratitude, creativity, and lightheartedness. Our poise disrupted, we become vulnerable, less effective and confused, distorting and misinterpreting what is happening to us – in a word, neurotic.

Our lost poise may be private, not easily discerned even by people in close relationship to us, or it may be overt, plainly obvious to anyone observing us. The life stories in this chapter reveal the pattern that we unconsciously repeat and then defend ferociously, even as it shatters our poise with complete predictability, and even as it keeps us stuck in our neuroses.

There are endless life situations in which people lose their poise, but there is one main trigger that ignites the largely unconscious process – self-pity. All of the examples in this book illustrate how we lose our poise when we feel sorry for ourselves. As you will see, once self-pity takes over our perceptions, we move inevitably into the rationalizations of victimhood and into a shrunken life.

Like most people, I have found it extraordinarily difficult to acknowledge my own self-pity. Self-pity is tricky, clever and deceptive, all barricaded ego, often hiding itself inside compelling victim stories that support and defend our thinking and behavior.

At one point in my life, I decided to recapitulate every time I lost my poise, beginning with the most recent and then working back in time as far as I could remember. I wrote down in my journal vignettes of every life disturbance – however brief or pervasive – that dislodged my equanimity. With each incident or example, I tried to remember the emotional content, thinking and behavior characterizing my state of consciousness when I lost my poise.

Here are some examples from my journal, beginning with the most recent incident from the time I began the recapitulation. It may not be obvious in each example, but self-pity triggers all of these incidents of lost poise.

- I was crabby with Mary about a minor household matter. In spite of her insightful analysis, feedback and coaching about this kind of pettiness over 16 years, I expressed some irritation with her, pointing out her lack of attention to something I wanted her to do. Mary has headlined this irritability of mine, "The Critic." Happily, The Critic is an infrequent and mild visitor these days. As I recalled the incident, however, I was flooded with memories of similar incidents – in my marriage to Mary and in my most valued relationships with others over my lifetime. Most of the people close to me have run into The Critic, and nobody has ever enjoyed my lack of poise at those times.

- Fed up with months of difficulties with a business partner, I confronted him with obvious anger and frustration. I heatedly gave him my assessment of his ingratitude, his lack of respectful communication, and his inability to work through business problems in a creative, productive way. He became very upset and stormed out, saying, "I can't take this. I quit." The partnership was over. Poised, I would have discussed, not accused; I would have been lighthearted, unattached to any outcome, rather than angry. With access to my love, I would have sought a creative solution – even, perhaps, the dissolution of our partnership.

- I had invested in a troubled teenage boy over several years, paying for half of his first two years of college and providing friendship and emotional support. As a weekend guest in my home, he rifled our belongings in our absence and drank enough alcohol to become obnoxiously drunk. Arriving home and seeing what had happened, I became angry. With lots of emotional intensity, I told him that he was no longer welcome in my home and required him to leave immediately. I have forgiven him, but we no longer have any contact.

• At a dinner gathering, one of our guests declaimed about his relationship with God, pontificating about the right way to understand our spiritual nature and detailing his own spiritual practices at length. I found his soliloquy pompous and his need to dominate the group's conversation self-absorbed and socially numb. Irritated, I interrupted and scornfully deconstructed his spiritual views point by point. The awkward silence that followed marked the end of the social dialogue that evening. It's easy to see now that I had lots of poised options. I could have congratulated my guest on finding meaning and happiness in his life. I could have artfully invited others to join the conversation and share their experience. I could have taken a bathroom break. But I didn't. I wasn't poised.

• I got a costly speeding ticket in the mail, with a photo of my stolid face behind the windshield, documenting once again my disagreement with speed limits. Irritated, I only half-facetiously told Mary that I consider Prescott Valley a fascist bastion, an unfriendly town I will avoid in the future. This memory reminded me of all of the other speeding tickets I have received over the years and the chip on my shoulder that appeared with each citation. I remember one winter Sunday night returning from a nearby small town to my rural home with a pizza for supper. There were no other vehicles abroad in that sleepy town, but I spotted the local constable on night duty, waiting on a side street for people like me to speed by. Suddenly his lights were flashing behind me, and – my pizza getting colder still 20 minutes from home – I pulled over. 37 in a 25. I was simmering as the officer returned to his car with my credentials and took what seemed an unconscionable amount of time writing the ticket. When he returned to hand me the ticket, he quietly asked, "Mr. Stokes, do you have any questions?" I said, "Yes, don't you have anything better to do tonight than lurking out here when there's no traffic?" "Well," he said, with great presence, I thought later, "I could also give you a ticket for not wearing your seat belt." With juvenile machismo, I said, "Go for it, if that will make you feel that you're ending this crime wave." Luckily for me, he ignored my stupidity, and we went our separate ways. Poised, I would have been present, obeying the speed limit to begin with, and avoided the entire melodrama.

• A non-profit agency hired me to lead it through a trans-formational change process. The CEO who had hired me, although committing a substantial amount of agency money and time to the change process and to me as key consultant, was ambivalent from the beginning about the change process. As a result, he sabotaged our agenda at several key junctures. He failed to show up at key planning meetings, signaling to his executives that this process was unimportant, Or he would say during planning meetings that he didn't believe in planning, leaving us all wondering why we were planning. Or he would not return e-mails and phone calls to me when I needed his assent or his participation in an activity.

I am aware of the challenges facing consultants in organizational change initiatives, and I expect difficulties. But, in this case, I found myself in a funk, somewhat depressed. I wasn't succeeding and the situation seemed to be worsening. In some meetings with the agency's leaders, I felt that I was the only one who wanted to move the organization forward. I never lost my composure with agency leaders in any overt way, but internally I was not poised. I obsessed about the problems and the leaders of the agency.

It was spring, and we had rented an oceanfront house for the duration of this contract, but I was unable to fully enjoy the beauty of my surroundings, unable to be fully present. I wanted to be grateful, but I wasn't. I wanted to be lighthearted but couldn't rise out of my funk. I complained to other consultants on my team, earnestly dissecting the agency leaders' ineptitude, attitudes and lack of energy. Usually creative, I couldn't think of anything else to do. And I certainly did not feel very connected to the agency's leaders; I was giving my best to get to know them, but they were withholding their trust from me, and I judged them to be weak leaders, unworthy of my respect.

Later, I woke up and stopped separating myself from the agency leaders with my judgments and self-pity. Finally, poised, I was able to complete the assignment successfully.

- I spent a full year off balance, depressed and sometimes resentful, when my wife at the time left me abruptly, catching me stunned and unprepared. Even though she lived independently following her exit, she generously gave me a full year to explore our relationship, participate in counseling and spend some time together. It was a year of semi-torture for me, however, living with my wife's ambivalence about our marriage and me. Even with my newly humbled willingness to examine myself, I was failing at reconciliation. I was the CEO of a dynamic, national organization whose people were accustomed to poised leadership from me, but I went off to work each day morose, struggling to lift myself out of self-absorption. By the time I walked into the office each day, I was able to present a façade of poise, but I did not convince my colleagues, who could easily discern my diminished energy and zest for life.

- By the time my recapitulation reached back over several decades to the incident I am about to report, I was clear about the single cause that triggered every incident of lost poise. By now I saw the culprit and could have ended the recapitulation, thus avoiding recalling this painful memory. But I will reveal it here, even though it makes me cringe bringing it to the surface again.

In my first professional career, I was a high school English teacher in a fading rural town of 600 people whose school was its most important asset.

A few months into my first year, I was lecturing in front of a class, standing close to the front row of students.

Sitting only a couple of feet in front of me was a lanky boy, J.B., 6 feet 2 inches tall, athletic and handsome. J.B. was an angry and aggressive kid, whose unhappiness was due to problems at home, according to faculty members who knew the family. School scuttlebutt had it for weeks that J.B. had been threatening to fight any teacher who gave him trouble. He seemed to be rehearsing an altercation with one of us, some dramatic physical showdown, a confrontation he predicted he would win.

As I continued talking, I looked down to see J.B. giving me the finger, making sure that his friend sitting next to him was witnessing the provocation. I stepped forward and slapped him in the face and then stepped back, prepared for him to come out of his seat. But he sat there stunned, a red mark on his cheek. I ordered him out into the hallway with me and threw my jacket on the hall floor, ready for battle. He stood there, furious, but passive. I took him to the Superintendent's Office and returned to my shocked class, all of whom had grown up with J.B. in this close-knit village.

My colossal loss of poise, terrible judgment and corporal punishment – the trade word at the time for this form of adult violence – did not end my teaching career, as it probably would today. J.B.'s parents complained to the Board of Education, demanding that I be disciplined, and a closed hearing was held one afternoon after school. J.B.'s parents met with the board privately, then left before I testified. I told the board what happened, without apology, as I remember. I don't recall any questions from board members, mostly hard-working local farmers, who listened soberly. After I left the hearing, they decided to take no disciplinary action against me. J.B. soon returned to class, and over the next two years, he matured, and we developed a respectful relationship. Neither of us ever mentioned the moment in which I was disconnected from our common humanity and my professional responsibilities.

THE UNIVERSAL PATTERN

When we lose our poise, a universal pattern of thinking and behavior is revealed:

1. The trigger of lost poise is self-pity. Challenged by somebody or something, we experience feelings of anger, frustration, irritation, resentment, fear, or some other eruption of emotional anguish. We feel sorry for ourselves.

2. Recoiling from these painful emotions, we instinctively reject what is challenging us in the fundamental sense that we believe what has happened or what is happening now or what might happen should not happen. Rejecting life as it flows in and separating ourselves from it, we instantly invent a victim story to justify to ourselves and others our rejection of what is happening and to explain how our painful feelings have been caused by someone or something else. Because we deny responsibility for the situation that triggered our anguish, it seems obvious to us that an external cause is making us feel bad.

3. Our poise now abandoned and feeling sorry for our-
    selves, we brood and stew, re-igniting our negative
    emotions over and over and keeping our victim story
    alive and metastasizing. We project our feelings onto
    a person or the persons we are convinced are the cause
    of our unhappiness. We obsess about them, rehears-
    ing our responses to them or making our case against
    them over and over in our minds, creating scenarios in
    which they get the punishment they deserve. We may
    plot revenge, even though this plotting fuels more suf-
    fering. We deny that we are creating this part of our
    life, that we are full participating partners in this awful
    dance. If I am cruel to others in my retaliation – even
    duplicitous – I rationalize my behavior, convinced
    that my tyrants deserve what they get back from me.
    At other times, I keep my anger hidden, and then I
    become depressed, suffering alone.

4. As soon as we create our victim story, we may try to
    get allies. We seek agreement and support from oth-
    ers that we are being victimized in this situation, so
    we tell our victim story with passion and conviction,
    hoping for rescue. We intuitively seek out others who
    will resonate with our victimhood because they see
    themselves as victims in their lives. If we fail to get
    agreement about our story from someone, we feel
    hurt and unloved and assume that others just don't
    get it, don't seem to have any empathy.

5. Trapped now in our victim story, going round and
    round in the eddy of our distorted perceptions, we con-
    tinue to defend ourselves inappropriately, and – stuck

and unconscious – we are unable to find our way back to poise. Our self-pity and our victimhood, if unexamined, are periodically reactivated, returning at regular intervals, a chronic virus that saps our energy and our confidence.

THE DIFFICULTY OF DISCERNING SELF-PITY AND VICTIMHOOD IN OURSELVES

Self-pity and victimhood are so pervasive in human behavior that we don't identify them as bad explanations for what is going on. Instead we interpret our anger, irritation, impatience, or fear to be sane reactions to elements of life we consider dangerous. We mistakenly embrace these emotional forces as part of our self-protection arsenal.

Human beings are fragile and require defenses to ward off injury to body and soul. We go too far in our self-protection, however, and build fortresses where they are not needed for survival. These seemingly innocuous and natural defenses become deep life patterns that prevent growth and learning. Self-pity and victimhood are the worst of our unnecessary defenses, even though we may claim to understand their limitations as a personal perspective.

> *The question of self-pity* ... We understand the aversion most of us have to "dwelling on it."... The very language we use when we think about self-pity betrays the deep abhorrence in which we hold it: self-pity is *feeling sorry for yourself*, self-pity is *thumb sucking*, self-pity is *boo-hoo, poor me*, self-pity is the condition in which those feeling sorry for

> themselves *indulge*, or even *wallow*. Self-pity
> remains both the most common and the most
> universally reviled of our character defects,
> its pestilential destructiveness accepted as
> given. "Our worst enemy," Helen Keller
> called it.
>
> Joan Didion, *The Year of Magical
> Thinking*

Self-pity is a major human strategy for explaining unpleasant emotions. It is not an emotion itself but rather a life
stance, a claim to some form of victimhood that places all of
the attention on me with no responsibility for my reactions
or decisions. Self-pity is a misreading of life, an inadequate
explanation for what is happening.

The storyline for self-pity goes like this: *I firmly reject what is
happening in my life right now, and I feel victimized because:*

- This is not what I'm entitled to.
- This is not right.
- This is not fair to me.
- This is not correct or just.
- This is not pleasant.
- This is not respectful to me.
- This is not properly considerate of me.
- This is not what I want.
- This is not nice.
- This does not recognize my importance.

As a life stance, self-pity and its cover of self-importance
are nearly impenetrable. Our "I-don't-like-this-and-somebody-

is-doing-something-to-me" storyline is not only our own personal default position but also a storyline everywhere around us – in our family, friends, workplace, society and world. We find support everywhere for feeling sorry for ourselves and blaming others for our anguished emotions.

The recapitulation of lost poise in my life shows me what a long half-life my own self-pity has had. Even after decades of warrior commitment to being humble and alert, I still had not disabled The Critic. Exposing my Critic as self-pity, for instance, was enormously difficult for me. Typically, I righteously believed that my criticisms of others should be understood as mere observations – valid, objective analysis of what others were doing.

Luckily, my wife, Mary, can tell the difference between my observations and criticisms. My objective observations and analyses don't hold a charge. But The Critic always delivers his analysis with a charge, an edge that betrays the underlying quarrel with life. The Critic is disturbed, however slightly and however subtly, irritated or angry at some level. The Critic says, in effect, I mind what happens in the behavior of others.

Below self-importance is self-pity in disguise. The victim story for The Critic is: I feel irritated, uneasy, because you aren't doing things quite right, so I have to correct you. Until you make the corrections you need to make, you will continue to make me feel dissatisfied, annoyed or worse. If you don't change, I may have to step up my criticism to a blunter level to get your attention. If you take too long to make corrections, I am justified in becoming cynical about you. My

Critic is the ego, which is hungry for the status of being right and being superior. This pattern is deep and difficult to unearth and acknowledge. To give up The Critic, I have to become aware of my emotions as they emerge, I have to take responsibility for them, and I have to say yes to what is happening in the moment – a radical shift in perception.

Another part of the pattern of lost poise is projecting negative emotions on other people, thus creating the victim story. My recapitulation reveals the pattern of blaming others for my troubled emotions in every instance of victimhood:

- My business partner is inept, unreasonable and unskilled, shortcomings that tortured me and caused my angry, critical response to him.
- The boy I helped through college is dishonest, disrespectful and ungrateful; his fatal flaws warrant my being upset.
- My pontificating dinner guest is boring, self-absorbed and socially ungraceful, requiring my petulant interruption and corrective speech.
- My student is disrespectful, hostile and aggressive, causing me to feel violently angry.

There may be no identifiable person or specific persons to blame for our loss of poise in some areas of our lives. Sometimes we project our disturbed emotions on faceless tyrants, like the government. I drive over the speed limit. I get caught. I'm disgruntled and feel sorry for myself. This should not happen to me. I should be able to go as fast as I want. I know what I'm doing. Why is my beautiful automobile built to go 140 mph if I can only go 70? I hate Big Brother and his cameras. Cameras are not fair in this game. I should not have to pay these stiff fines. My insurance should not go up. I should not have to spend all day Saturday in traffic school. The tyrant is the government. Who can blame me for being upset when I have to contend with unreasonable authority?

This particular pattern plays out every day in our society's endless victim stories about government. The television news commentator invites us to respond to his poll, "What are you angry about with our government?" tacitly approving our self-pity by inviting us to register our out-of-control emotions online. Anger and blown poise have become the required credentials to enter the political dialogue in some venues. If you're not angry in those circles, if you're not ranting, you may not have an audience in the political debate. Unfortunately, for a large proportion of our citizenry, the victim-story is the default explanation of choice about all problems in our society.

GAINING ALLIES FOR OUR VICTIMHOOD

Naturally, we want support for our claims to victimhood and loss of poise. We tell our victim stories to people close to us, hoping for agreement and validation.

During the period of my painful separation from my former wife, the victim story I told family and friends focused on how hard I was trying to confront my own flaws and how she was avoiding confronting hers. Yes, I admitted, presenting myself as a paragon of self-awareness and fairness, I contributed to the problems of the marriage, but she was not owning up to hers. Was I to accept all the responsibility for the failure of the marriage, I asked, reasonably. I must shamefully admit now that I shared intimate details about my wife's unacceptable behavior, to make sure that my friends and family knew just how difficult it had been for me, the sad, abandoned, victim husband.

My recapitulation reveals that in every incident of lost poise I sought allies for agreement and support. The retelling of my victim stories to sympathetic people gave me a moment of comfort, but also etched my self-pity more deeply. My explanations for what had happened were not accurate readings of reality. But frequent repetition of these bogus rationalizations locked in my distortions, making it more difficult for me to discover alternate and more accurate explanations in which I take full responsibility for my feelings and the life I create.

VICTIM TRIANGLES AND SELF-DECEPTION

The most powerful support that we can build around our victim stories is the victim triangle, a dynamic in which we allow or recruit someone to actually enter the fray with us, standing shoulder-to-shoulder in victimhood against the tyrant who is making us feel bad. The victim triangle is populated by:

- The central victim whose suffering propels him to create and tell the victim story
- The rescuer of the central victim
- The tyrant – the real or imagined person or entity who victimized the central victim.

The central victim feels anguish in some form, then projects his pain onto the tyrant. He tells his victim story to the rescuer, who is so sympathetic that he enlists in the cause, deciding to help, to fight for the victim by joining in the virtuous battle with the tyrant.

We create these dynamics unconsciously, so we usually don't even notice them playing out in everyday life. Our victim stories become a cover and justification when we lose our poise. My friend, Gayle, tells this story about the last time she lost her poise, an incident in which she volunteered for the rescuer role without being recruited.

> My fifty-year-old daughter hadn't been feeling well for some time, and I finally insisted that she go to the doctor. I accompanied Hanna to her doctor, who sent her to the hospital for further tests, the beginning of a harrowing day for both of us. The hospital physicians informed us that Hanna had cancer in her kidney. They made an appointment with an oncologist, and we saw her that same day.
>
> Waiting in the oncologist's office, my very worried daughter said, "Mom, you're so calm." Actually, I was terrified. When the oncologist reviewed the test results with us, she said that this type of cancer is difficult to treat. Her diagnosis was that Hanna had a short time to live – maybe six months. Stunned and upset, I pointed out that there was still a test

result in the laboratory that the oncologist had not yet seen. The doctor replied that she had sufficient data for her diagnosis and said, "I'm confident about my analysis." I was enraged and said, "Fuck your analysis!" We left the office shaken and frightened, and I was determined that we not accept this diagnosis.

That was eight months ago. Hanna's kidney has been removed, and the diagnosis is more hopeful now, even though she still has cancer and an uncertain future.

Gayle believed that this story illustrates that, yes, admittedly, she lost her poise, but ultimately she felt justified to object, to be upset and angry, understandably hostile. The tyrant in Gayle's victim story is the oncologist whose diagnosis, Gayle believes, was premature and incorrect. Gayle makes her daughter the victim, of course (even though we have no evidence in the story that Hanna feels like a victim). Gayle is the rescuer, standing up against the blunt, unfeeling, and incompetent medical world.

Many people will sympathize with this interpretation of what happened, siding with the image of a caring, no-nonsense mother defending her daughter. But it is a flawed and distorted explanation, as all victim stories are.

The only real culprit here is Gayle's anger and her self-pity. This shouldn't be happening to her daughter, she believes, and it should not be happening to her, so she rejects life in the moment and projects her anger onto the doctor.

If we want to be poised, we must understand experiences like this one. It is easy to be deceived by victim stories. They are seductive to our egos and our own self-pity as they attempt to gain our agreement. On the surface, victim explanations may seem true, even though they are always distortions created to gain sympathy, status or self-justification.

A BETTER EXPLANATION

How is Gayle's story false – a distortion – and what would have been a better explanation than the victim story Gayle created, an explanation that would have allowed Gayle to remain poised?

First, Gayle's emotions at hearing the diagnosis – anger and fear – are unconscious, irretrievable and personal. Another mother might not have any hint of fear or anger in the same moment, supremely aware that we are all going to die and, unafraid of death, able to hear and discuss this diagnosis with perfect poise.

But emotions are personal and surface without our beckoning them. They interact with the world but need not determine the world or determine our response to the world.

In this case, a poised Gayle would have recognized her initial emotions for what they are and consciously avoided creating a victim story. Instead, she would have remained present in this poignant moment, connected to her daughter and connected to the doctor, rejecting nothing and embracing life as it flowed in.

She would have called on her gratitude, thankful for having her daughter alive today and for the period ahead. She would have been grateful for the doctor's knowledge and life commitment to healing.

Poised, Gayle would have been creative, exploring with the doctor the possibility that yet unexamined tests might reveal new evidence. She would have explored a second opinion. She would have asked about the most expert treatment centers for this type of cancer or about new treatments under study. Poised, she would have guided her heart to be light, allowing her love to flow into this moment, keenly aware that life is precious and finite.

Because Gayle's victim story is beguiling, we might on first hearing believe that it documents a mother's love. But Gayle did not have access to her love. She accessed only her self-pity and, abandoning her poise, made the situation worse. The greatest price we pay for lost poise is not having access to our love – not being able to call it up when it is needed, as it was in this moment.

THE SANCTIMONIOUS RESCUER
In victim triangles, both the central victim and the rescuer lose their poise. The lost poise of the rescuer, however, is disguised. The rescuer may pretend to be poised, but – like the person she is rescuing – the rescuer has separated herself from life and from other people – the bad guys against whom she makes her stand. Not connected, she hides her own self-pity behind the sanctimonious mask of doing good, as illustrated in this example.

My consulting firm was facilitating a change initiative in an organization, when two employees of the organization privately complained to a relatively inexperienced member of my consulting team about some organizational shortcomings they felt were victimizing them. They told my colleague that the top executives in the organization were treating them unfairly. They were angry and bitter, they said, about a consistent pattern of incompetent management of their project and biased treatment of them personally. Disgruntled employees frequently confide in outside consultants about their negative assessments, hoping to influence changes they want, and my colleague, flattered by their confidence, was easily drawn into their victimhood.

Instead of asking the two employees to take responsibility for their anger and bitterness and to pursue their grievance with the organization's leaders, my colleague moved into rescue mode, her own self-pity resonating with their emotional anguish. Trusting her more now, they revealed that they had enlisted fellow dissidents to take their project out of their organization – a mutiny of sorts.

That evening I received an emotional call from my colleague to report on this victim story, which she considered an injustice to the two employees. The organization's leaders were obviously less than competent and ethical, she said angrily. She felt that we should have an urgent concern about these employees and their valuable project. She had become the rescuer, and now she was on a righteous mission.

The executives who had engaged our services enjoyed a sterling reputation for integrity, but now, based only on the victim story she had been told, my colleague assumed the worst about them. She had not asked the employees if they had ever voiced their concerns with top management. They had not, it turned out.

After hearing my report of the incident, the organization's leaders met immediately with the two employees, listened to their concerns and negotiated changes that would reduce tension, build better communication and improve project performance. Both employees stayed with the project and improved its performance in a stronger partnership with management.

Rescuers in victim triangles are susceptible to the self-pity and victimhood in themselves, thus the victim stories of others resonate powerfully with them. In the role of rescuer, my colleague's ego was fortified, her sense of self as a brave defender of the oppressed strengthened. Angry, she lost her poise, abandoned her professional judgment and exacerbated the problem.

Even after the issue was successfully resolved, she was unable to acknowledge her error. Simmering unseen below her rescue was her own self-pity, which continued to distort her perception of the situation.

VICTIMHOOD IN ORGANIZATIONAL LIFE

As the previous example illustrates, our workplaces offer the perfect dynamic needed for self-pity, victimhood and lost poise. Power is embedded in positions in the hierarchy.

Those with lower positions in the hierarchy are vulnerable to decisions made by those above them. Those with more power can set compensation, assign work, evaluate personal and professional behavior, give promotions or terminate employment.

It is a universal tendency in the workplace to view those in power as flawed, unsympathetic or even duplicitous, thus organizational leaders often become tyrants in the minds of unhappy employees.

When employees develop a victim story to explain their unhappiness – rather than seeing their situation as a challenge and making decisions to address the challenge – they often recruit colleagues for sympathy and validation. Thus victim triangles are ubiquitous in the workplace, draining energy and lowering morale, creativity and productivity.

A friend tells about his supervisor, who regularly presses his buttons of self-pity and causes him, he says, to lose his poise. He describes his supervisor as brilliant, generally effective and neurotic. Even though the boss is basically loving, even tender some of the time in response to human problems, he also is easy to anger and frequently expresses his frustration caustically when his standards aren't met. My friend recognizes the self-pity and victimhood in his boss and understands how he produces a victim story when he is dissatisfied with something.

The boss's victim story, which everyone in the office knows well, according to my friend, is: I have very high standards, and most of you don't. You don't seem able to get things done properly and on time. You are making me angry. I am well justified in my exasperation and ire. Expressing my displeasure toward you is simply a professional intervention to get you to raise your standards of performance. It's my job.

My friend and his office co-workers react to the boss's periodic anger and harsh, confrontational approach with their own victim story. They complain about the boss behind his back and exchange fantasies of flight. My friend confesses to his own victim story: he feels sorry for himself, arguing that he should not have to put up with abuse. The boss can be a tyrant, setting staff on edge, making them shut down and retreat into passivity, he reports. He says he is intimidated by his boss's intellect and unpredictability and believes that the boss is responsible for his ambivalence about his own job. My friend decides to quit in protest every few months, even though much of the time he likes his job.

None of the people in this familiar workplace dynamic are poised. Self-pity frames everyone's perceptions, and the victim stories distort reality. All of the players blame someone else for their angst, but no one takes any responsibility or creative initiative. Instead, in order to make a living, they believe they have no choice but to slog on.

An innovative workplace of the future might do well by providing training to line staff, managers and leaders on how self-pity produces victim stories and on how to sustain poise when relationships are challenging.

VICTIMHOOD IN THE FAMILY

Loss of poise is commonplace in the family environment, of course. In families where self-pity and victimhood ripen with every hurt feeling and disappointment, members lose their poise frequently. When anger, frustration and impatience shape the dynamics of relationships, family members do not have their love at their disposal and the purpose of the family – to love, protect and develop its members – cannot be fulfilled.

Notice how this story from my friend Faye illustrates clearly each step of the universal pattern of lost poise:

> Growing up, I never felt loved by my mother. She never seemed to approve of me completely or even be very interested in me. My older brother could do no wrong with her, and I always resented her obvious favoritism. So I became the difficult daughter always contesting her authority.

> In adulthood, I continued to feel unloved by Mom. Although we have always had frequent contact, I have never stopped being angry and resentful toward her. She loved my son and poured affection on him for fifty years, but I never felt her approval myself. I have had long periods of depression in my adult life, and I feel that the lack of my mother's approval could be a big explanation for it.

My defense with Mom was to be cold and non-responsive. In recent years, Mom, now in her 90s, has tried to reconcile. She frequently asked, "Please tell me what is wrong. What have I done to make you so unfriendly toward me? Please tell me so I can make things right." I always said that nothing is wrong and that there is nothing to do. Then she would cry.

I have always talked to friends and family members about how my mother drives me crazy. Over the years, I've complained plenty about Mom to my brother, who continued to have a very loving relationship with her. He has always urged both my mother and me to reconcile, but neither of us changed. She continued to act the victim with me, and I continued to feel victimized by her.

When she went into hospice a few months ago prior to her death, I visited her often to do my daughterly duty, even though I didn't feel generosity toward her. I cleaned out her apartment and disposed of her belongings. When I told her what I had done, she became very upset that I had not consulted with her and burst into tears of anguish. As usual, I just felt that she couldn't acknowledge any of the many things I did for her. My brother, aware of this last melodrama, urged me to make peace with Mom before it was too late, but I probably just retreated further from her, refusing to give her my love. To be brutally honest, I don't miss having Mom in my life.

Faye was not poised in her relationship with her mother. She isn't really present with her mother, unable to welcome their interaction even with death approaching. She obviously is unable to feel connected, even in the sense of a common humanity.

Faye is not grateful, maintaining instead her lifelong complaint. Her creativity is used mostly to maintain her distance while appearing to be dutiful and to frustrate her mother by refusing reconciliation. She is unable to be lighthearted, her bitterness weighing her down. As in every case of lost poise, love cannot be accessed.

The universal pattern unfolds predictably in this story:

1. Faye feels anguish, anger and resentment.

2. She has created a lifelong victim story: Mom has never loved me and that reality has caused me to resent her and to protect myself from her. She prevents us from being close. Mom causes me anguish.

3. Faye feels sorry for herself. She keeps her victim story alive for over five decades. She is cold and sometimes cruel, rationalizing that her mother deserves it or that she needs to protect herself.

4. She seeks allies for her victimhood from family and friends. When her brother suggests a different approach, she refuses.

5. Faye's victim story is a bad explanation for what is happening, but she is trapped in it. Unable to understand how her self-pity is strangling her love and her capacity for forgiveness, she cannot find her way to poise.

LOST POISE AND THE UNRESOLVED ISSUES OF MARRIAGE

It goes without saying that we are most likely to lose our poise in our closest relationships. In marriage, for instance, we often establish patterns of losing our poise nearly every time certain unresolved issues reappear. Maury Povich has created a daytime television hit by showcasing the blown poise of his guests – screaming and crying angry spouses and lovers –willing to air their deepest anguish in front of millions of laughing observers.

But most married couples or partners are ashamed when they lose their poise with each other and want to keep it hidden from others. In the privacy of their homes, good people can get into very deep ruts with each other, recreating the same scenes over and over, abandoning their preferred poise for default patterns of anger and suffering.

An acquaintance tells this story of a pattern of lost poise in his marriage:

Nan and I married young, high school sweethearts, and have three children now ten years into our marriage. Our relationship has been volatile from the beginning. Even in the first year of marriage, something I'd say would set Nan off, and I would have to deal with her rage and crying without ever understanding what was going on.

Nan never forgets a wrong, imagined or real. In any argument, she can bring up examples of my errors and transgressions from years ago. I object to bringing the past into the present, but she is relentless in making her case against me when she is angry and out of control. Then good times return until we repeat the cycle of fighting once again.

Nan says marriage is "two against the world," but I disagree. I feel that we should have friends and embrace the world. As it is, we have no friends. Every time we socialize with another couple, I face Nan's groundless jealousy and wrath when the evening is over, because, she says, I've been "too friendly" with the other woman.

I've thought for some time that Nan is mentally unbalanced and, not to my credit, I frequently tell her she is crazy when she becomes enraged. I plead with her to stop fighting in front of the kids, but the more I plead, the more she escalates the battle. The other day I escaped one of these horrible scenes by retreating into the bathroom and locking the door. In front of the kids, she pounded on the door for several minutes, screaming, "I hate you! I hate you!"

We never solve our problems or sort through our differences. We never learn anything that helps our marriage improve. We never change.

TO BE POISED, WE NEED GOOD EXPLANATIONS

Many married people will recognize themselves in some elements of this story. The unresolved issues of the marriage keep cycling back predictably, reigniting anger and self-pity. Nothing changes much, the victim story of each partner obscuring the truth and blocking any honest examination of the unresolved issues. Neither spouse is learning anything.

The husband's victim story admits only indirectly to his negative role in the marriage dynamic, but ever so reasonably builds the case to find Nan guilty of the marriage failure. Nevertheless, his is a distorted explanation for what is happening, as all victim stories are.

What is preventing a breakthrough in this marriage is not differences over issues, although those exist – as they do in all marriages. What prevents any learning in the marriage is the absence of poise.

Poised, this couple could talk about any problem, learn together and put issues behind them permanently. Poised, they could enjoy the process of resolving problems. Poised, they would have access to their love every hour, every day. Sustaining their poise, they would present to their children a successful adult relationship full of caring, respect, creativity, and fun. Poised, they would be able to see the other person as a magical being with unlimited potential. Poised, they could have a real marriage.

For this marriage to be successful, both partners will have to acknowledge their self-pity and the bad explanations that emerge from it. They will have to commit individually to becoming poised so that they can bring their love fully into their relationship.

LOST POISE, VICTIMHOOD AND BAD FAITH
Feeling sorry for themselves, victims and their rescuers operate in bad faith. They don't feel powerful enough to take full responsibility for their lives, so they create petty tyrants, abusers or bad guys to explain their impotence and suffering. They may mistrust people they perceive to have more power than they do, so they say what they think the powerful person wants to hear, later telling other victims what they really think – that the bad guys are doing something to them.

In spite of their bad faith, victims paradoxically attempt to level the playing field by claiming moral or intellectual superiority over the bad guys. Victims never tell the whole truth because their victim story is a distortion to begin with. Instead, they distort the facts, data, experience, and information to make a case for their own virtue.

Poised, we operate in good faith. Poised, we don't project our anguish onto others but take joyful responsibility and credit for the life we are creating. Poised, we recognize the self-pity in ourselves but avoid giving it any validity. Poised, we don't invent victim stories, aware of their fundamental abandonment of integrity.

Poised, we don't feel helpless or impotent. A warrior always has alternatives. Poised, we are life-creating marvels.

WHAT ABOUT PETTY TYRANTS WHO ARE REAL BAD GUYS

But aren't some victim stories true? What about the vicious people who murder, rape, or commit other brutal crimes? Aren't our victim stories about them true? Isn't it true that they are vicious tyrants and aren't their victims, well, victims? And aren't these victims in need of rescue?

Fortunately, most of us in the Western world don't have to defend ourselves directly from sociopaths or psychopaths. Most of our personal tyrants are itsy-bitsy, teensy-weensy petty tyrants in a warrior's perspective.

But truly vicious and unscrupulous people exist, and they may pose a threat to another's life or fundamental well-being. If someone wants to kill me or a loved one, or if someone steals my wealth, or if someone intentionally plots to undermine or harm my health, my family, or my employ-ment, isn't it valid for me to explain all this with a victim story in which there is a real bad guy, there is a real victim and there is a real need for rescue? Isn't this story the best explanation for what is happening?

VICTIM STORIES ARE BAD EXPLANATIONS

No, the victim story is never the best explanation. Even in the case of real bad guys, this explanation is still the flawed story of self-pity, a story that cannot be transformed into truth, no matter how difficult our challenges may be.

> We now recognize that if there is anything at all that can bring us down – anything – our house is built upon sand and there is fear ... Thus we become motivated to confront the places in ourselves that bring us down – not only to confront them, but also to create situations in which to bring them forth.
>
> Ram Dass with Stephen Levine,
> *Grist for the Mill*

In other words, my challenges are my path of learning, and I must go in search of them.

To be a victim is to turn away from the transformational learning that only challenges can make possible. The only person who can turn me into a victim is myself, and I can do that by rejecting my life, projecting my troubles onto someone or something outside myself.

My victim story presents me as essentially impotent, a leaf at the mercy of the wind. On the other hand, all a warrior has are his challenges and his decisions, and that is enough. As a warrior traveler on a path of love, I can choose to squeeze self-pity out of my decisions.

This insight is difficult to manifest in real life when confronted with severe challenges.

In the example of Bernie Madoff's infamous bilking of investors out of billions of dollars, the media used the word victim over and over in telling the story. In many televised interviews with financial investors who lost large sums in Madoff's Ponzi scheme, many used the word victim to describe themselves. Most of them told a typical victim story: they were angry, devastated, shocked, incensed. This evil man had betrayed their trust, and now they had lost a fortune – in some cases everything. Many demanded rescue. Wall Street had failed them. The government regulators had failed them, and they should get their money back. Some wept in the retelling of their victim story.

Most of those interviewed were absorbed in self-pity, but a few investors responded with considerable poise: they were, they said, investors responsible for their decisions. They admitted they had deluded themselves when they believed that Madoff's unusual returns on investment were possible – returns substantially higher than any ordinary and legitimate investment in the marketplace. They acknowledged that they should have been more skeptical and less greedy.

In other words, contrary to the victim story in vogue in the national consciousness, they took responsibility for their losses, learned something about themselves, and moved on, poised.

POISED AT THE EXTREMES OF HUMAN SUFFERING
Even in the most wrenching examples of human suffering,
some people avoid the victim role.

We have ample evidence from history that some people are
able to retain their humanity under the most horrific of circumstances, a humanity that requires extraordinary poise.

Viktor Frankl, in *Man's Search for Meaning*, the classic report
on his experiences in the Nazi death camps of World War
II, gives examples of poise achieved by prisoners. In telling
about a camp where prisoners died every day from starva-
tion, illness, murder, or loss of will to live, Frankl praises
his fellow prisoners who were able to achieve presence, connectedness, gratitude, creativity, and even lightheartedness.

- Presence: In a daily life that was brutal, frightening, and
  bereft of hope, some prisoners had moments of presence,
  moments of poise, in which they did not reject life. As their
  inner life became their only escape from suffering, Frankl
  reports, some prisoners appreciated the beauty of art and
  nature as never before: "In camp, too, a man might draw
  the attention of a comrade working next to him to a nice
  view of the setting sun shining through the tall trees of the
  Bavarian woods (as in the famous water color by Durer)."

- Connectedness: In the midst of his own soul's anguish,
  Frankl says he became connected to his fellow humans
  in a new and profound way. He saw that *"The salvation
  of man is through love and in love. I understood how a
  man who has nothing left in this world still may know
  bliss ... in the contemplation of his beloved."* He thinks

of his beloved wife, not knowing that she herself has died in another camp, realizing for the first time the ultimate meaning of love residing within himself. And, even though he rates his own response to terrible suffering as mediocre, he volunteers as a doctor to care for typhoid patients in another camp, a duty that was likely to hasten his own death but at least end his life in service to others.

- Gratitude: Prisoners were able to feel gratitude for "the smallest of mercies." Any moment free of suffering was noticed and appreciated. He is grateful for a fellow prisoner, the only cook who dishes out the daily bowl of soup without looking at the prisoners in line, not favoring his friends over others. In another incident, he remembers the luxury of a few days in the sick ward, where, even though they were given less bread and soup than prisoners who were working outside in freezing temperatures, he and his ill comrades could lie all day pressed together in relative warmth in a hut and sleep.

- Creativity: Creativity was a survival necessity, like learning to stay on the inside of a formation of prisoners because those exposed on the outside were often beaten mercilessly and without cause by the guards. But the greatest creativity of the prisoners was tapping their inner riches, the memories of their past lives, which were a refuge from their emptiness and desolation. The prisoner's "memory played with past events . . . In my mind I took bus rides, unlocked the front door of my apartment, answered my telephone, switched on the electric lights . . . These memories could move one to tears."

- Lightheartedness: Frankl tells about training a fellow prisoner how to laugh, getting him to promise to invent at least one amusing story each day about some incident they could imagine after liberation. Frankl believed that lightheartedness is part of mastering the art of living, and he practiced it in the concentration camp even though severe suffering was never absent. From time to time, after the day's labor, prisoners created a semblance of a cabaret, entertaining each other with singing, jokes, and poems in order to have a bit of life-giving laughter.

The powerful lessons about poise to be drawn from Frankl's experience begin with his confirmation that we have a choice about our encounter with suffering. Some of his fellow prisoners chose not to take advantage of the opportunities presented to them in suffering; "they did not take their life seriously and despised it as something of no consequence." Others, "the mediocre and half-hearted," failed to turn this experience into an inner triumph and simply vegetated.

Emotion, Frankl believes, is suffering, but ceases to be suffering if one can come to understand it. Only a few on his fellows were able to transmute suffering into inner liberty and the highest moral behavior. These were the individuals whose love and compassion did not dim during their own great suffering, individuals who gave away their food when they themselves were starving, individuals who found the hidden opportunities in suffering. Rising above their outward fate, Frankl observes, these people prove that it is possible for us to achieve spiritual greatness.

Frankl, who did not number himself among the few great souls in the camps, has moments of exultant victory over his suffering:

> I was trying to find the *reason* for my sufferings, my slow dying. In a last violent protest against the hopelessness of imminent death, I sensed my spirit piercing through the enveloping gloom. I felt it transcend that hopeless, meaningless world, and from somewhere I heard a victorious "Yes" in answer to my question of the existence of an ultimate purpose.

For a moment, self-pity is defeated, life is embraced fully, and poise is achieved.

4

Sustaining Poise

To finish the moment, to find the journey's
end in every step of the road, to live the greatest number of good hours, is wisdom.
Ralph Waldo Emerson, *Selected
Journals*

Great rewards await those who move intentionally toward
sustained poise. Good hours fill each day. More and more
poised, you spend more and more time in the present moment
and less time rehashing the past or worrying about the future.

In sweet poise, your cup is filled to the brim, and you move
gratefully into each precious moment. On the path toward
greater poise, your heart lightens with each step. When you
are able to sustain poise, your creativity flows naturally,
finding solutions for every problem and engaging every
potential. Poised, you have full access to your love. Poised,
you are a magical being exploring magical universes.

You can become fully poised, as others before us have become fully poised. What does that state of consciousness look like?

First, fully poised, we are still human beings who have challenges. We still have things to learn, but fully poised, we are able to anticipate our next level of development, understand the likely challenges ahead, and move into the future, eager to learn. We don't need any excuses. We aren't tempted to blame anyone else for the life we are creating but, instead, are happy to acknowledge our creative responsibility for every moment. Life is rich in wonders, and our lives can expand without limit because we live in an infinite universe. We are capable of taking everyone into our heart's embrace. We feel one with the earth, our great mother. Tuned in to what wants to emerge, we acquiesce to life and feel united with our true selves, at last.

Until you are able to sustain poise, however, you are vulnerable. Your explanations, your ideas and theories, about what is going on with your troubles with certain people or with certain situations, are inadequate. You continue to repeat the same responses, even though they fail to resolve the challenges you face. You continue to lose your poise whenever these challenges predictably cycle around again, even though you have tried to avoid the challenges and even though you have tried to be poised when these difficulties show up again. This is what it feels like to be stuck.

Moving from your current state of consciousness to sustained poise is a transformational process, a personal evolutionary leap. The good news: many intrepid seekers have taken this leap. You can make this leap to sustained poise yourself. This chapter presents a transformational map.

CONFRONTING SELF-PITY

To sustain poise, we must be free from acting on our self-pity. As long as we can feel sorry for ourselves for more than a moment, we will lose our poise some of the time. As long as we can be offended – as long as we need to fortify our self-importance – our poise is ever vulnerable to the behavior of others. As long as we tell victim stories to explain how life is treating us badly, we will struggle unsuccessfully to be present, connected, grateful, creative, and lighthearted. Locked up in victimhood, we are stuck in our own dead-end creation and will continue to stumble every time certain challenges test our poise.

To find our self-pity, we don't have far to look. It is, and always will be, close by. To find it, we merely have to list the situations in which we lose our poise, the times we argue with life, wishing it were different from what it is.

This first step toward a more sustained poise looks easy, but it is difficult. Our minds want to argue that it is normal and necessary to reject certain elements of life, as the victim stories in this book testify.

The mind insists that rejecting people and situations that obviously make us unhappy or unsafe is the sane thing to do. Of course, I should and must reject being unfairly accused. Of course, I reject being abused. Naturally, I reject being cheated. Shouldn't I reject being ill? I believe effort and diligence should be rewarded, so I expect positive outcomes.

Aren't I entitled to getting what I deserve? And isn't it normal to be depressed when the people around me don't seem to see the real me and don't seem able to love me?

IDENTIFYING WHAT WE REJECT ABOUT LIFE
Hopefully, the list of people and life situations that we reject is a relatively short one at this point, but we need to know what is on the list. Make the list now.

- Who disturbs you? Name the individuals or groups and describe what it is about them that you reject. Who haven't you forgiven?
- What situations disturb you? List them and identify what you are rejecting in these situations.
- What are the triggers for your anger, irritation, and impatience?
- What can make you unhappy? Is there anything that can throw you into a funk or even depression?
- What are you afraid of? What do you avoid, even though there is no imminent danger?
- What outside yourself would you like to eliminate from life? What about life seems imperfect to you?

Now you know what makes you feel sorry for yourself currently. You have identified the domains for losing your poise, and you know where to begin your work on your self-pity, the fuel for all of your rejections of life and ultimately the fuel for all of your bad explanations about what is going on.

Your brave acknowledgement of your self-pity and the various defenses you've invented to project your unhappiness onto others is a breakthrough in awareness.

RECAPITULATING LOST POISE

An even deeper understanding about our historic patterns of self-pity and lost poise can be achieved with the recapitulation strategy discussed in the previous chapter, a strategy inspired by Carlos Castaneda's profound warrior learning regimen and adapted here to examine our personal history of lost poise.

In the tradition of learning from the shamans of ancient Mexico, recapitulating every life experience is partly a quest to lift the imprint of socialization by examining its dominating effect in every moment of life. For those ancient shamans, recapitulating life experiences was a path to freedom and an evolutionary leap available to any person willing to make the investment.

To engage this powerful strategy, write down every incident of lost poise you can remember, beginning with the most recent and working back in time as far as you can remember. Meditate on each incident, remembering as much detail as you can. Remember the people, the place, the situation. Remember exactly how you lost your poise. What were your negative emotions at the time?

Recapture how you were unable to be present in the moment, the degree to which you were disconnected from other people and from life generally, how you lost access to your love. Try to remember how you lost your gratitude and the degree to which you felt you didn't have enough. Look for the absence of creativity in your response to what was happening. What was your mood and how heavy was your heart?

You will remember more and more detail as you move down the list. Look for the wounded self-importance in each experience. Look for the self-pity. Remember the victim stories you concocted with each incident of lost poise and how flawed they were as explanations for what was happening. Bring each incident of lost poise back to life so that you can feel it again. Relive each incident.

In each case, notice what you were rejecting in your life at that time. You may discover that you no longer reject some of the things you rejected previously in your life. You have learned about yourself, and you have changed. You are no longer thrown off balance by certain behaviors in others as you once were. You no longer have the same sense of entitlement you once had. You can laugh at yourself in ways you weren't able to earlier in life.

In my own case, I noticed that since childhood I have tended to lose my poise when I thought I was being disrespected. I have a history of lost poise in situations where my self-importance got pricked. In each case, my self-pity was activated because I felt others didn't treat me respectfully, and I instantly created victim stories – bad explanations for what was happening.

Because of my recapitulation, I am now able to spot self-pity's weak demand for attention when someone does not show me the respect I want. Bemused, in the moment, I recognize it as an old ghost, groveling for my attention. I refuse to give it any legitimacy, and it fades quickly into the background as I move back into the stream of life, poised.

This strategy pays huge dividends, worth every hour devoted to it. The process of recapitulation may itself produce gains in awareness, and it is less likely that you will repeat some of your patterns of lost poise in the future. You may emerge from this recapitulation more humble, more alert, and more able to laugh at yourself, letting go of the past and welcoming the future and anything that it brings to you. It is possible that you will enjoy a more sustained poise.

But it is probable that you will discover patterns of self-pity and lost poise that require further examination and learning, patterns that are current and unresolved. Your clarity about these patterns of lost poise is more powerful now, and you are ready to let them go for good.

LEARNING STRATEGIES
We can learn to sustain poise. The speed of our learning will depend on the quality of our learning relationships and our willingness to open up to what we are rejecting about life. Once we have done some self-assessment and have identified the elements of life that we reject – the people and situations that align with our lost poise – we need some learning strategies.

There are some strategies that we can pursue alone. We can quiet our minds through meditation, prayer, and exercise. We can gain helpful new knowledge from books and other sources.

But even if we have a strong desire for change, we won't be able to alter our thinking or our behaviors substantially without another person or persons supporting us and learning with us. We might prefer to be able to make personal breakthroughs in awareness with heroic self-discipline and determination, but we cannot.

What about reports from people who claim solitary spiritual epiphanies, which came literally in a moment and transformed their lives forever with profound new insights and clarity?

Many people have written books about these kinds of experiences and report convincingly that their old ways of thinking and behaving were suddenly vanquished and that a dramatic expansion of awareness emerged into their lives from that moment on.

Some credit their emergence to terrible suffering that seemed to set the stage for the breakthrough, like Viktor Frankl's experience in the Nazi death camps that led him to see that life has meaning. Drugs have been the stimulus for breakthroughs in human awareness. Prayer and meditation, of course, have been sources of insight, and many report direct, personal instruction from God about what to believe and what to do. Don't these experiences prove that we can, indeed, achieve transformational change alone?

No, they don't prove that these strategies – pursued alone, without engaging anyone else as learning partners – will produce sustained poise for anyone who tries them. In our quest for poise, we need good explanations. The stories of epiphanies fall short as good explanations of how to achieve poise or any other state of consciousness. The people who report extraordinary, sudden breakthroughs in awareness do not exist alone. They have families, friends, neighbors, teachers, co-workers, and lovers.

Even if they claim a solitary epiphany, they have lived with and been influenced by people their entire lives, making it difficult to credit one moment in their learning or an unearned victory as the cause of their transformed consciousness. They may have seen everything with a startling new clarity in a moment, but a lifetime of experience and learning with other people set the stage, contributed to each stage of learning and, finally, what appears to be an epiphany.

All significant gains in awareness are the result of rigorous self-examination and difficult learning. Gains in awareness are hard-earned. And we can't skip levels of development, but instead must get a foothold in each stage before we move to the next stage. Epiphanies that seem to contradict the laws of human development are bad explanations.

Nevertheless, learning strategies that can be pursued alone should be added to our menu as we pursue sustained poise. One or more of them might work to some extent for you. Experiment.

And find a learning partner.

WHEREVER TWO OF YOU ARE GATHERED
The most powerful strategy we can pursue in our quest for sustained poise is engaging with a committed and loving learning partner.

We need someone to help us learn because we need chal-lenging feedback about our blind spots, our habitual ration-alizations, bad explanations, and life-limiting behaviors. We need someone who can see our potential, even when we do not see it ourselves. We need someone who has a stake in our life, someone who not only sees what we might become, but whose life is affected if we continue to lose our poise.

We need someone to give us encouragement, someone who will celebrate our victories and successes with us. We need a learning dialogue with someone who is seeking to learn the same things we are seeking to learn. As learning partners, our dialogue must be intimate, nurturing and challenging, a dialogue that will clarify where we are stuck and that has the power to unearth strategies for sustaining poise.

Our spirits joined, we pioneer as a scouting team on the fron-tiers of human emergence.

The most likely candidates as learning partners are prob-ably already in your life. Learning to sustain poise requires a learning partner who is trusted, an intimate friend of your well-being. This person could be your spouse, a lover, a close friend or family member, a minister, a psychiatrist or counselor, a mentor, a co-worker.

Perhaps the person is not in your life yet but will soon appear because you are ready and will make room in your life for this significant relationship. Perhaps you will have more than one learning partner but what follows assumes that you will recruit one key person to join you in pursuit of transformation.

THE EXCITING PURSUIT OF POTENTIAL

Moving from a habitual defense of self-pity and victimhood to sustained poise is a personal transformation, the most difficult level of change that we can tackle.

We live in an age of transformation, writer Peter Drucker believed, an age in which all human organizations, institutions and systems are engaged in large scale change initiatives in order to adapt to the dynamic advances of modern life. As members of these systems, individual men and women are struggling to learn how to transform personally in order to contribute and thrive in the new human dynamism. The individuals who are not engaged in transformation are at a great disadvantage, their learning skills and relationships inadequate to the challenges of adaptation.

Individuals who are able to contribute to the new human dynamism have in their skill set the ability to assess their own awareness continuously in partnership with other vibrant learners. Thus, the most invaluable element of the modern person's life is a network of fellow learners, at the center of which is a small number of intimates and most often one person who is a fellow warrior traveler, our chosen partner in the exciting discovery of potential.

We have been drawn together by energetic forces we cannot discern, as if the universe matches us up to do the work of awareness. These special relationships are the most important relationship in our lives. No one else will know us better than this person because we are working together on the frontiers of our emergence as human beings. We expose our weaknesses to each other. We listen deeply and help each other see where our life explanations are incomplete or inadequate.

Together, we continuously develop better explanations and test them until we find explanations that enhance our consciousness and accurately predict the outcomes of decisions and new directions. We love each other, and we will continue to love each other as long as we see potential in each other and remain committed to pursuing that potential.

STAYING AWAKE

It takes considerable consciousness and discipline to create and sustain learning relationships aimed at transformation. Daily life demands our attention and energy. Our jobs take much of the day. There are groceries to buy and the house to clean. The family needs us. We should exercise, and we'd like to have some fun.

We become immersed in a busy life, of course, but we can help each other stay awake by reminding each other of our real agenda – to become more aware. Then, as Ram Das says, all daily life is grist for the mill rather than a distraction or a set of requirements. Everything we do is an opportunity to be poised.

We have several key ways to help each other avoid drifting into unconsciousness, where we repeat our patterns of self-pity, victimhood and victim stories.

First, we can help each other sharpen the case for change, the set of reasons that our current level of poise is not acceptable. Maybe:

- I lose my poise all too often. I find myself angry.
- I get impatient or depressed when I don't get my way.
- I can't seem to find a common humanity with certain kinds of people.
- I don't always have access to my love when it's needed.
- I can't quiet down enough to be close to nature some of the time.

We are not satisfied with our own state of consciousness. We are not satisfied with our partner's state of consciousness. In our dialogue, we identify the thinking and behaviors that must evolve if we are to sustain poise. We uncover together our self-pity and victimhood. We deconstruct our victim stories and acknowledge them for what they are – bad life explanations.

With liberating truth-telling about how we lose poise, we create a necessary disequilibrium and discomfort for ourselves as the intimate dialogue exposes how we are limiting our lives when we lose our poise. Trusting each other, we are able to shake things up. This is love in action.

Second, we can help each other develop an individual vision – a preferred future in which we sustain our poise. We describe in detail what living in sustained poise is like. Our vision will be challenging and difficult to achieve, but it also will be highly attractive and desirable, describing thinking and behavior that will enhance life in every moment.

The case for change	My vision of a poised future
I lose my poise all too often. I find myself angry pretty regularly. I feel sorry for myself sometimes when challenges test me, and I lose my poise. I feel separate from certain people in my life and spend quite a bit of time obsessing about them, rehearsing some comeuppance or even revenge. My anger is accompanied by violent thoughts sometimes, even though I abhor violence and don't commit it. My anger is damaging some of my relationships with people I love.	I understand my self-pity as the cause of my anger, and I'm able to catch it in the moment. Whenever I experience anger rising in me, I notice what I'm rejecting in life and, instead of acting on my displeasure, I am able to be present in the wonderful now, connected and grateful. I don't need to fuel my ego with anger, and I don't need to project my quarrel with life onto somebody else. I'm able to call on my creativity when something needs changing, and my light heart allows me to enjoy life, even as I face challenges. I'm simply bemused by what used to upset me, and now I sail free, a warrior traveler, looking, looking, breathlessly. Accepting everything in life, knowing that everything is perfect, I am poised.

Building a vision together, we bring excitement and commitment to a state of consciousness full of joy, harmony and love.

Our vision will stretch us and motivate us. It is a statement of our optimism and faith in each other and ourselves.

Our vision sets our direction, giving us the capacity to see ourselves from an altitude well above the vicissitudes of everyday life.

FREQUENT DIALOGUE

You and your learning partner must talk frequently about the challenges you face and the progress you're making or not making as you confront your self-pity. This strategy seems obvious, and yet most people do not have an ongoing dialogue with anyone about their growth and development, let alone anything so ambitious as sidelining self-pity and sustaining poise.

To get a measure of how difficult it is for people to understand these profound issues, ask yourselves how many people you know who have successfully navigated this transformation. It may appear counter-intuitive to most people in our lives to constantly scratch the scabs off our wounds and to deconstruct our hidden life, our rationalizations, and other defenses. In our case, however, mindful that we are opening ourselves to a more flourishing life, we are willing to examine our self-pity, even though it is a humbling and painful process at first.

But our dialogue will not be entirely focused on the challenges: much of the time it will be light and humorous. It also will be life-giving as we celebrate the fully poised times we achieve. We will delight in our new capacity to catch negative emotions and self-pity as they arise in the moment and also our new suppleness at choosing a creative path in the face of challenges. We will become more poised, and we will gain confidence as we learn. As we become a powerful learning team, our dialogue gives us unequaled advantage over any solitary strategy. Our learning relationship will become the top priority of our lives.

You will likely have other relationships in which the issues of poise can be raised. Family, friends and colleagues will benefit from what you're learning with your partner, and you will invite them into the dialogue to the extent they are interested and able. You and your learning partner will create an expanded learning environment for yourselves. At the least, you will be carrying your poise into every interaction with others, who will be drawn to you at a new level of trust. Everybody around you will gain from your increased poise.

UNDERSTANDING THE VICTIM STORY AS A BAD EXPLANATION

With your learning partner, you have a case for change. You know you want to derail your self-pity. You have a vision of sustained poise, a level of conscious behavior that you have not yet achieved.

One by one, the people or situations that you reject must be invited back into your lives with a new explanation around them. This new explanation can only be achieved when we abandon the bad explanation we use currently – the explanation that protects our self-pity and victimhood from scrutiny. The problem for the ordinary person, however, is that self-pity is so beguiling and seductive as an explanation for what is happening. It is all too easy to project our inner state onto our environment.

Taking full responsibility for what is happening in any moment is a radical shift of life interpretation.

Most of us have been socialized to accept the victim story as a good explanation for what is happening when we find ourselves in emotional discomfort or anguish. We have used our victim stories perhaps thousands of times by now to explain our emotional disturbances and to mask our self-pity. Our life has had two sides: One is the relatively happy side, when we feel that life is treating us well; the other side is the unhappy side, when we feel that life is not treating us well, the part of our life we reject. Our victim stories are our explanation for what is happening in the latter, unhappy part. They make it impossible to sustain poise.

The trouble with victim stories is that they are always inadequate explanations for what is happening. They may provide a temporary relief from our anguish, as we convince ourselves how beset we are by life's unfairness, but actually they don't work. If victim stories worked, they would be helpful in identifying things to avoid in life. Avoiding those things, then, would move us closer and closer to happiness.

Here's an example:

A man marries his high school sweetheart. In the first year of marriage, he is horrified to discover that his young wife is frequently angry at him. She is jealous and questions where he has been and with whom. Her shrewish response to him makes him question himself, so he tries to be perfect for her.

He picks up his socks and shorts, gets home on time for dinner and tries to be affectionate and understanding, but nothing works. They quarrel constantly. He is miserable and on edge, dreading the next attack; she seems always angry with him, and he can't figure out how to please her. Ultimately, he decides she's crazy.

He becomes attracted to another woman to whom he confides that his wife is crazy and cannot be pleased no matter what he does. His new friend is loving, sexy, calm, a joy to be around, and they have an affair. He is happy when he is with her, apparently the complete opposite of his wife. This is his victim story. He divorces his wife and marries his lover.

He is now free of his first wife, the woman he is convinced made him unhappy. If his victim story is a good explanation of his unhappiness in his first marriage – in other words, if his first wife was the cause of his despair – he should now, away from her, be happy.

But he is not. His second wife begins to question his love for her. She doesn't seem so delighted to be with him anymore. She doesn't yell at him like his first wife did, but she seems to harbor a chronic irritation with him. She has some strong beliefs he doesn't share, and there is frequent tension between their life views.

He begins to believe that his second wife had hidden her true self from him during their affair and before their marriage. She seems to him now to be a different person. She begins to say things like, "Now I see why your first wife was always mad at you."

He drifts away from her, spending more and more time with friends, to whom he presents the explanation for his unhappiness with her: she is not the person he originally met. He says that she must have been on her good behavior to reel him in, but now that she has him, she reveals her true self – a rigid, opinionated person always ready for argument.

He is a normally cheerful person, he says, but she has made him depressed and anxious. Marriage itself becomes his new petty tyrant and the culprit in his revised victim story, and he acts on it by divorcing for the second time, vowing to live life as a single man. He is convinced that his victim story is a good explanation for what has happened and believes he will be happy if he simply avoids marriage in the future.

But he is not happy. Single again and living alone, he tells his friends that he has concluded that marriage is a failed institution: it makes everyone miserable because it is an unnatural state. Better, he says to be a free man, doing what he wants when he wants to do it.

He goes out with single women for short periods until he sees signs that they are looking for marriage; then he pulls away from them and tells friends that he is not about to be trapped again. All women are nice until they're married, he says, then they become something else. Women may not realize what they're up to, he says, but he sees through them and he sees through marriage.

Yes, he admits to some limitations in his new lifestyle, but it's better than being fooled again.

This is his new victim story.

VICTIM STORIES ALWAYS LIE

The man's self-pity and victim stories fail him as explanations for his life at every turn. They do not recognize his responsibility for the relationships he creates with women. They do not predict how he can be happy in the future. They do not give him insight into what he might learn that could help him become happy. Instead, his victim stories block his ability to understand himself better.

What's on his list of things he rejects? He rejects women, suspicious of their good will, sanity and integrity. He rejects marriage as a partnership that could create more love, comfort and healing. He rejects the possibility that he is the cause of his failed relationships.

He feels sorry for himself and creates victim stories to explain his failures. The more victim stories he develops over time, the deeper his self-delusions, and the more he limits his future. His bad explanation becomes his life.

What is a good explanation of what is happening in his life, an explanation that could help him see how he is creating his own life, that could identify needed learning, and that could begin to chart a path toward successful relationships with women?

The beginning of a good explanation, free of self-pity and victim stories, might go something like this:

> I have not learned how to relate to women successfully, even though I am very attracted to them and enjoy their love and affection. I have been divorced twice and haven't been able to create a long-term relationship with any of the women I have dated since. I feel sorry for myself.

Or, if he has more insight:

> I have not learned how to relate to women successfully, even though I am very attracted to them and enjoy their love and affection. Once we make deeper commitments, however, I am unable to understand their needs. I am unable to love them after the initial sexual excitement and easy fun. I am unable to hear their feedback to me; I get confused and then begin to retreat if my efforts to please them don't pay off right away. My attacks on women and marriage are all bravado to cover up my inadequate capacity to love. I have escaped into a fairly cynical bachelor life to protect myself from being hurt. I feel sorry

for myself and make up victim stories. I have
not yet learned how to sustain poise in intimate relationships.

This beginning of a good explanation of what is happening
will be painful, but it is a scrupulously honest self-examination that could be the first step in transformation, testing new
approaches and improving his explanation about women as
he learns.

In the good explanation, he accepts responsibility for himself, blaming no one else. He acknowledges that he has much
to learn about loving women. He can predict future failures
with women if he doesn't change. If he follows through and
learns how to love women, he will be able to expand the
good explanation, one that will be life-giving. He will stop
rejecting the most important things in life and begin to sustain poise.

DEVELOPING GOOD EXPLANATIONS

Replacing bad explanations with good explanations is the
path to sustained poise. It is an exciting process of expanding
our consciousness with our learning partners. The process is
very difficult, however. Our self-pity has riveted us to the
bad explanation. We still feel sorry for ourselves, even as we
begin the process of examining our self-pity. Deconstructing
our bad explanations threatens us, leaving us feeling naked
and vulnerable because we haven't yet developed a better
explanation that serves us in times of challenge. Our bad
explanation is the only way we have had at this point to
understand what is going on when we resist something that
is happening in our life.

The good explanations to be developed will be radically different from the bad explanations that we have relied on so far. The radical shift comes when we take full responsibility for both what is happening and how we are reacting.

THE RADICAL SHIFT
In the bad explanation, I feel sorry for myself because I believe that someone or something in my life is causing me to feel distress. Someone or something outside myself is doing something to me. I feel that I am a victim to an external force and that I must reject what is happening and build a defense against it.

In the good explanation, I feel sorry for myself when I feel distress, and for a moment I may want to reject this part of my life. But I don't reject it. I embrace it and accept full responsibility for what is happening. External forces may threaten my well-being, but I welcome what is happening because only then can I make use of the opportunity presented by this problem. I refuse to be a victim. I will call this distress a challenge and bring my full warrior poise into the moment, relishing the undisputable fact that this is my life right now. Present, connected, grateful, creative and light-hearted, I am impervious and say yes to my life in this moment.

Moving from bad explanations to good explanations may be the most difficult process of learning that we will encounter in our lifetime. We're giving up a life view that has helped us cope, however inadequately. It's the life view we've been taught and practiced. It's a life view shared and supported by many people around us. Giving up self-pity and victim stories does not intuitively feel correct.

THE STAGES OF DEVELOPING A GOOD EXPLANATION

In your dialogue with your learning partner, you will be able to deconstruct your bad explanations and move to good explanations that set you free for a buoyant life of joy and practical advantage. Knowing in advance the stages of learning ahead will equip you to be successful with the rigors of letting go of self-pity and victimhood. Here are the stages you and your partner will inevitably move through:

Stage One—Confronting Self-pity: You're losing your poise over something that is disturbing you right now. You tell your learning partner about your distress, your anger, irritation, or fear. You present a bad explanation—the victim story in which you reject a part of your life, blaming someone or something else for what is distressing you. You are the wronged star of this melodrama, and you wouldn't mind having some sympathy, agreement and support. Maybe you would like to be rescued. You are convinced that you are reading this situation correctly. You are certain that you are losing your poise because of someone or something that you can't control. You think that you have a good explanation.

Your learning partner rejects your victim story as a bad explanation, pointing out correctly that you are creating your emotional discomfort. At this early stage, it's very difficult to understand that this might be true, so you resist your partner's interpretation. You develop your victim story even further, with greater detail about the obviously unfair challenges you face from outside, assuming that your partner is not quite understanding your dilemma. Your partner still doesn't buy your victim story and encourages you to look for your self-pity in this situation and how you're inventing a victim story to deflect your own responsibility for your distress. You don't find this exchange pleasant and may find your partner unsympathetic or even dense.

Stage Two—Deconstructing Bad Explanations: Your learning partner encourages you to try retelling the story as if you are the sole creator of your lost poise, blaming nobody and nothing outside yourself for your anguish. Giving up the victim story entirely proves to be a difficult assignment, and you stumble with it on your first try. You may take some responsibility for the situation in your new narrative, but you probably continue to blame the people and situations outside yourself for what is going on. You agree that you have lost your poise in this situation, but it simply does not seem true that you would create this kind of trouble for yourself.

Your partner may retell the story as if you are responsible for what is happening in your life, so that you can hear what a good explanation sounds like. In your partner's version, there is no victim, just you feeling sorry for yourself, rejecting part of your life and projecting the responsibility onto people and the world outside yourself. You are responsible for losing your poise. Your partner's version seems ruthless, and you may find yourself defending your disturbed emotions as healthy and necessary—certainly human. You wonder why your partner can't see the obviously flawed people and world you have to deal with. You're on the defense, because your partner's version describes you in unfavorable terms.

With more dialogue, you begin to admit that you are responsible for your life, but the process is painful. This is no fun.

Stage Three—Taking Responsibility: With lots of dialogue, you begin to be more skilled at creating a good explanation. With encouragement from your partner, you make a breakthrough—developing a good explanation about what has disturbed you.

> I have lost my poise in this situation because I feel sorry for myself. Yes, I am creating my own life every day, every moment. Yes, when this circumstance confronted me, I blamed the outside world for my lost poise. I was unable to be present, connected, grateful, creative or light-hearted. My lost poise took me down a path that has not been successful. I made whatever challenges I faced worse with my self-pity and victim story. Because my victim story is a distortion, a bad explanation, I made mistakes. I made myself unhappy. I shrunk up my potential. I lost access to my love. This is what really happened, and I am beginning to realize that this disturbance is a pattern of mine. I am humbled by this realization.

Now you are able to imagine how you could address this situation in a new and dynamic way, poised, taking responsibility for the life you're creating. You and your partner create alternative scenarios that you might create and explore, scenarios in which you are joyful and gain the maximum practical advantages from what is happening. You are beginning to glimpse a life in which you can move self-pity into the background when it appears. You are beginning to see that life need not be restricted or reduced or refused in order to protect yourself. You are feeling chagrined about what you have failed to be aware of in the past, but the new possibilities are exciting and you sense an emerging liberation from self-pity and its bad explanations.

Stage Four—Practice: With your good explanation, you are more poised. Even though the original challenges you face are still present in your life, you see them in a completely different way. You welcome them, as Lao Tzu's masters of awareness welcomed all things. You feel present, connected, grateful, creative and light-hearted. You make some changes immediately. You approach the people and situations that have been challenging you in a new and creative way, taking full responsibility for what happens. You may be amazed that the problems that plagued you seem to disappear altogether once you stop feeling sorry for yourself.

You realize that you need to test your new poise, so you look for chances to practice. You look forward to people and situations that used to prick your self-pity and self-importance so that you can manifest a good explanation. And, indeed, they show up quickly, and you are delighted to find yourself sustaining your poise more and more effectively. You may slip up sometimes, but you stay with your practice, making the most of every test.

On one glorious day, something challenging presents itself, something that used to throw you into distress, and for a moment you feel sorry for yourself. But in the next moment you remember everything you have learned. You consciously move self-pity into the background, and you sustain your poise artistically. You have discovered the vibrant life of the warrior traveler.

Stage Five—Poised, Humble and Alert: Poised, you have gained a new level of personal power, an ability to mobilize your energy in the moment. You feel that you are the master of your life. You have a new buoyancy of spirit and a new confidence. Life is good.

And then you discover that you can still slip into subtle forms of complaint about life. You can still allow self-pity to seep in, and then you object, however mildly and reasonably, to some challenge that life brings you. Periodically, you are unable to embrace fully what life is presenting. Sometimes you mind what is happening.

You and your partner can help each other detect and deconstruct these nuances of self-pity and victimhood. There's more to learn and more practicing to do. We may never achieve a perfect poise, so it's best to maintain a warrior's alertness and humility. Overall, though, we are supremely aware that we are among the most fortunate of beings.

MARY DEVELOPS A GOOD EXPLANATION

My wife, Mary, and I have gone through all of these stages as learning partners, looking, looking breathlessly, warrior travelers pioneering on the frontiers of our own emergence. It has been my great good fortune to have Mary's skilled and loving learning partnership, even though I resisted like everyone else does in the early stages of our investigation into my bad explanations. Luckily for me, she did not give up on my potential, even in the face of my stolid resistance at times.

Here Mary shares how she went through the five stages of developing good explanations when she found herself losing her poise in a predictable pattern several years ago. Mary labels her story The Irate Customer:

>Stage One—Facing Self-pity: As a consultant to large corporations, I developed a training program for sales people about understanding customers and their needs. I created a training program called "The Buyer's Mind," which was used to train thousands of sales people. It turned out that my high standards for customer service became a problem when I was the customer.

>I felt sorry for myself as a customer when a business didn't meet my service standards, and I created a victim story to justify my irritated and quarrelsome confrontations with representatives to get what I thought I was owed as a paying customer. I blamed large, distant corporations for impersonal and unresponsive service, especially if I had

to navigate Byzantine phone service systems, only to reach a representative who lacked authority to solve the problem or who didn't seem to be responsive and competent.

This pattern of irritation eventually troubled me, but I continued to defend my bad explanation every time I lost my poise. Gary would hear me berating a business representative on the phone if the representative didn't correct a billing mistake quickly, for instance, and question me about it later. He pointed out that I was losing my poise pretty often in these situations. He suggested that the company representatives didn't create the system, but merely carried out company policy. I was wedded to my victim story, though, and defensively suggested that maybe he'd like to take over the bill paying.

Stage Two—Deconstructing Bad Explanations: A turning point came one day after I hung up from yet another exasperated phone attempt to straighten out a billing problem with a company representative. I had lost my poise, indulging in impatience and irritation to make my complaint. When I hung up, Gary said, "I don't suppose the people who have these customer service jobs come to work every day looking forward to talking to irate customers who come on the line ready to do battle."

Suddenly my bad explanation, which depersonalized the phone representatives, was exposed as I imagined real people doing a difficult and probably modestly paid job. For a moment, I saw that I had been creating battles and creating needless tension and unpleasantness.

A good explanation began to emerge in my dialogues with Gary. Gradually, and somewhat reluctantly, I recognized that I had made phone representatives the faceless bureaucratic enemy, that I was waging mini-wars, and that I was creating negative outcomes for myself and others. My self-pity arose when my complaints weren't immediately rectified. Whenever the irate customer was in play, whenever I felt angry or irritated, there was a subtle victim story operating just out of sight. This was a profound realization for me.

As I gradually was able to take full responsibility for my irritation and unpleasant approach and own up to the reality I was creating in these calls, I was humbled. I think of myself as a cheerful, generous and tolerant woman, but the victim in me looked pretty stupid and unaware. This process of learning was challenging and painful.

Stage Three—Taking Responsibility: I was able to bring my emerging good explanation into play the next time I had to get a problem solved. I carefully avoided the irate customer persona and talked to the representative like I talk to most of the people in my life — with calm respect. The problem was solved quickly, and I enjoyed the conversation.

That easy success helped me nail my good explanation for the irritation I had been feeling in these situations. The good explanation: I mistrust large corporations. When I have problems with them, I feel sorry for myself because I believe my rights and needs are not respected. I'm convinced they don't understand the buyer's mind. I actually am an expert in how buyers think, yet, in the middle of this strength, is my blind spot. I didn't fully understand my own mind.

I create a victim story with the corporation as the tyrant I must battle. I am fierce with them, because I don't trust them and believe I have to fight for what is right. In the process, I question the motives and the integrity of the representatives of the company. I treat them badly, even as they try to solve the problem for me, which they almost always do eventually.

When I talk to the representatives, I am not present, welcoming all things, obviously. I am not connected, but instead act as if the person on the other end of the line is barely human. And I'm not connected with myself, my values of respect, love and kindness. I'm not grateful for my many blessings, but instead earnestly focus on what I don't have but feel entitled to. I misuse my creativity to outmaneuver my adversary, an adversary I have invented. Needless to say, I'm not light-hearted, but earnest and one-dimensional. Most of my assumptions have been wrong, and I now reject the bad explanation. I am responsible for creating these unpleasant situations.

I am on new ground, taking full responsibility for blowing my poise. I have made a radical shift.

Stage Four—Practice: I was excited, because I was now passing every test of my poise when I had to get a business problem sorted out over the phone. Representatives were meeting the real Mary Morris now, and I was enjoying these conversations with total strangers. And all the problems got resolved by competent, pleasant employees on the other end of the line.

Then, just when I felt it was permanently relegated to the background where it couldn't darken my perspective any more, the shadow of my old self-pity fell into my life again. I returned a Christmas gift, and was told by the salesperson that I could only get half the original cost back because it was now on sale. I felt emotions rise in my body, which let me know that I was resisting life and might lose my poise. Aware in the moment, I quickly concluded the transaction and left the store.

I sat in my car for a moment, amazed that I was so close to once again playing out the irate customer. Sadly, even though I kept myself in check, externally poised as I concluded the transaction, I realized that I had been unable to keep a pleasant look on my face. This let me know that I didn't have complete access to my love. Had I been more aware in that moment, I would have realized that I am the author of my life. I created this situation. I could either argue with life as it was in that moment or not. I decided not to, but my face betrayed a hidden resentment.

Then, though the incident was over, the tug of my mind to replay the familiar victim story was almost irresistible. I was struck by how deeply I wanted to dramatize my sense of injustice and how difficult it was for me to resist.

Because of my dialogues with Gary, I knew that this seemingly small incident was an opportunity for me to deepen my expression of poise. So, to interrupt my usual patterns, whenever the merchant's face appeared in my mind, I thanked her sincerely for giving me an opportunity to practice being poised. During my drive home and even into that night, I thanked this merchant many times and, triumphantly, avoided the victim drama. Indeed, a victory! Obviously, at the time, I was not at the point of "I don't mind what happens," but I was able to interrupt a pattern in the moment and make a poised choice.

And next time I'll keep a look of love on my face.

I began to take the lead in my dialogues with Gary about what I was beginning to see as my larger patterns as an irate customer of life generally. I saw that my self-pity has been playing out in a subtle way throughout my life, and irritation with others has been my predictable emotional response when I felt life disappointing me. I realized that my self-pity had fed a low-grade irritability whenever my sense of entitlement was thwarted. In other words, the irate customer of life showed up anytime life didn't deliver what I thought I was due.

Stage Five — Poised, Humble and Alert: I have pledged to bring poise into every moment, taking full responsibility for the full shape of my experience. There can be no complaint from now on, only a joyful "Yes!" out here on the frontiers of human emergence.

Nevertheless, I am aware that self-pity floats in and out of my psyche like an uninvited ghost. Our worst enemy, indeed, as Helen Keller said. I'm still capable of shrinking into a smaller self for a short period, before I snatch my poise back from danger. I'm still capable of earnestness and a boring repetition of my old irritation. I can sense eons of human suffering continuing to reverberate through my nervous system, even though I would like to make an evolutionary leap into the beginning of a new human narrative.

At the moment, though, I am present, connected, grateful, creative and light-hearted. I'm poised, humble and alert.

ERASING YOUR BUTTONS
We often hear people repeat the cliché, "You know how to press my buttons," which means that someone knows how to make you lose your poise.

In other words, I have emotional vulnerabilities – self-pity, self-importance and victimhood – that are quite obvious and predictable. You know how to get me to lose my poise by poking at my weak spots and so you have a great deal of power over me. Yes, I lose my poise when you push my buttons, and it's your fault. I'd be fine if you weren't so unconscious, careless, and cruel with me.

"You push my buttons" is another bad explanation for what is going on.

Mary's story is about sustaining poise in the next moment after her buttons are pushed and she feels self-pity. Even though we can reduce self-pity to some extent through experience and learning, we will, as I have said previously, always have self-pity because it is an integral protection used by our species. But we are capable of identifying self-pity in the moment, checking its influence and diverting it to the background.

This isn't repressing our emotions: it is bringing consciousness to our emotions and making decisions about what happens next. In the next moment, then, we take full responsibility for charting a course, even in the face of great trial, and move into the situation whatever its challenges, poised.

Have we eliminated our buttons? Not exactly. We still may have an uncomfortable moment when certain situations arise. But our initial emotional response is not granted any decision-making power. With a lot of dialogue with our learning partners to identify our "buttons" and our self-pity, we can come to see ourselves with bemusement and more easily test new responses.

The first time we keep our self-pity in check in a situation that usually provokes it, we have made a move toward personal power and freedom. Ah, I say, when someone says something disrespectful to me, there it is again. I feel the discomfort: My self-importance just got pricked, and I see the self-pity under the disguise of my self-importance. Ah. And then ha, ha!

No victim story emerges because I am conscious, observing my patterns. Yup, saw that one a few hundred times in my recapitulation, and I'm ready. Victory. Success!

CONTROLLING OUR FOLLY

All human behavior is folly. My life is folly in the sense that none of my cherished beliefs, commitments, behaviors, or achievements is important in any permanent way. All will be swept away at death.

Much of the time we live in a bubble of self-perception, able to see only reflections of ourselves. So we talk about ourselves endlessly, propping up our egos, telling our life story over and over as we gaze onto our reflection.

Seeing only ourselves, we create folly.

We repeat our personal history so often that almost anyone who knows us can predict with confidence what we will do next.

Rick has told us repeatedly what his political predilections are, how his family has always been loyal to a certain party, and how dissatisfied he is about the current administration. We're pretty sure how Rick will vote next time.

Becky has told us often about how frightencd she is of flying in airplanes, how she panicked the last time she flew, and how she never wants to fly again. We're pretty sure that Becky won't be leaving on the next flight.

Alex likes to tell us often that he hates physical exercise, vegetables and fruit. He isn't interested in his negative body mass index and, he says, he plans to live in the fast lane as long as it lasts. His health future isn't much of a mystery to us, and he is not a mystery even to himself.

We're not poised when we talk about our lives so compulsively and predictably.

As we sustain poise more consistently, we will naturally let our personal history wither away, avoiding gluing our personal narrative together again with each retelling. To control one's folly requires observing our repetitious, predictable thinking and behavior. We can let go of all of our ego's props.

Our egos aren't worth perpetuating. As we stop feeding our egos, less and less of our precious energy will be soaked up by our personal narrative, a creation of the past, gone now and forever, except for our devotion to it.

Then we will move permanently into the now, where we will be present, connected, grateful, creative, and lighthearted.

Poised on a loving path and living outside the bubble, we control our folly.

A STATEGY: PREPARING, DOING AND REVIEWING

To ensure focus and discipline, you and your partner can use preparing, doing and reviewing as an outline for your dialogue about self-pity.

This ancient learning strategy is powerful, but it requires discipline and a commitment with your learning partner to manifest the strategy consistently. For those who do, learning is speeded up. The strategy is simple, but it is a way to uncover good explanations for what is happening.

A daily preparation may be sufficient. Each day write down what you intend to achieve that day. For instance, you might intend to watch for the situations that prick your self-importance and self-pity and end in your irritation and sour and cranky behavior. You plan to catch it in the moment and react with grace, humor and creativity – poise.

You go into the day conscious and intentional, pursuing everything you need to do that day, but doing everything in a larger frame of consciousness. The day will be even more interesting than normal because you have a secret purpose that heightens the significance of every encounter.

At the end of the day, or tomorrow before you plan again, revisit your written plan. Did you stay awake? Did you remember your purpose? Did you notice your irritation when it arose and did you adopt a new mood in the moment?

Some days you will forget. Some days you will remember and enjoy the victory of overcoming your historical patterns. If you find that you become lost in the events of the day, your preparation may have to be revisited during the day. At lunch, pull out your plan and recommit. Maybe you'll need to do it every hour for a while. Do whatever you have to do to stay awake.

Even if you prepare and remember, you may still fail to derail the irritation and continue to blow your poise. You've been irritated for a long time and your habits may prove stronger and more impervious than you realized. Your victim story is more resilient than you guessed.

Your intent will have to elevate to a level that will overpower old patterns. You literally may need to devote each day entirely to waking up to your irritation. Everything you do and everything you think about may have to move through the gauntlet of your vision of sustained poise. The first person I encounter today: Here she comes; I will not be irritated (even if you're never irritated with that person). After that encounter: how did I do? Hey, I was cheerful, poised. Next person . . . and so on.

When preparing, doing and reviewing becomes the agenda for the dialogues between you and your learning partner, you will share your plans and reviews and give each other tips and encouragement. This strategy has built-in accountability: your partner is not going to enjoy hearing you say that you forgot your plan day after day. We need to expect each other to bring our plans into manifestation and bring back valuable learning.

In my experience, most of our entrenched patterns will give way to this strategy. Over time, you will interrupt your irritation in the moment. You will drop your victim story, replacing it with a good explanation about what is happening in your life when other people don't do what you want them to do.

As you experience the practical advantages of not minding what is happening, when you are able to embrace whatever is flowing in, you will be able to move to a higher level of creativity – a level where you choose your mood at all times. You will choose to be poised.

TAPPING THE UNSURPASSED VALUE OF PETTY TYRANTS

Poise is a state of consciousness that can be tested and sustained only in the challenging arena of real life, surrounded by other people. As Ram Dass points out, the monk meditating for 30 years in a mountain cave may have achieved a profound quietude, but that poise will be disrupted as soon as he enters New York City and all of his uncooked seeds get exposed.

But most of us are not isolated and solitary, and so our disrupted poise happens in our interactions with others. I have always laughed at Jean-Paul Sartre's definition of hell as other people. But at times we may feel that we are, in fact, in hell with certain individuals and groups.

Imagine living in East Germany after World War II with the insidious Stasi, the state security organization that recruited neighbors, co-workers, and even your family members to spy and report on you. If you questioned the state in any way, you could be harassed, ostracized, imprisoned, or killed. The state was the smothering brutal tyrant, an unusual opportunity to test and develop one's poise that is difficult for us to find in our relatively benign political reality, as we will see in this discussion.

The use of the term "petty tyrant" is borrowed from the work of Carlos Castaneda, whose teacher, Don Juan Matus, encouraged him to seek out petty tyrants in order to confront and defeat his self-importance and self-pity:

> Self-importance is man's greatest enemy. What weakens us is feeling offended by the deeds and misdeeds of our fellow men. Self-importance requires that one spend most of one's life offended by someone.
> Carlos Castaneda, *The Wheel of Time*

Other teachers, philosophers and psychologists have understood the horror of spending one's life offended by other people. Petty tyrants, people who seem intent on harming us, are a necessary asset in confronting our victimhood and its resulting loss of poise. As Ram Dass was quoted earlier, we must seek out whatever brings us down.

But nothing could be more counter-intuitive to us than to seek out people we believe should be avoided – avoided because we are convinced they are the source of insult, emotional suffering, and serious harm. These petty tyrants seem to be a threat to our well-being, and our instincts for survival kick up when these people enter our environment or when we become obsessed with them – even though they are not physically near.

Now, however, we can use petty tyrants to test and sustain our poise.

WHO ARE PETTY TYRANTS, AND HOW DO WE MAKE USE OF THEM?

Petty tyrants are creatures of our imagination, in the sense that we believe they are doing something to us. We give them a huge role in our lives when we see them as personal enemies. We worry about them. We rehearse – sometimes obsessively – how we will deal with them, how we will handle or defeat them, or how we will push them out of our lives.

The petty tyrants in our life may not actually be interested in us at all and may not be doing anything unusual in their relationship with us. The banker, for instance, turned down our loan request, and now we feel offended and feel the victim of the uncaring banking system. The applicant turns the banker into his petty tyrant.

One of my rural neighbors tells me he is angry with the federal government because he can't get access to assault rifles and ammunition for assault rifles. Actually, he can purchase that weaponry, but my neighbor is convinced that the government is a threat to his ability to defend his home and family by considering gun control of any kind. He sees the government as a tyrant in his life.

On the other end of the spectrum, some petty tyrants actually want to harm us and do it intentionally and systematically. There are real thieves, muggers, scammers, rapists, and murderers, after all.

Why call real bad guys "petty" tyrants? The answer is that we are making a transformation from victimhood to sustained poise, and we want to shrink the significance of problems that other people seem to present, partly by laughing at them and ourselves. Thus, "petty tyrants" or "teensy, weensy, itsy-bitsy petty tyrants" remind us humorously that the challenges posed by other people are trivial compared to the power of our own creativity and the breadth of our consciousness.

As long as we think that somebody is doing something to us, we keep alive our invention of the tyrant, and we will continue to see our poise evaporate when a troublesome person shows up.

In sustained poise, we are delighted to accept full responsibility for the life we are creating, including the people and situations that we want to reject. Poised, I cannot be a victim; I have only challenges and my decisions. Troubling people that, in the past, I allowed to bring me down are now opportunities to overcome self-pity and self-importance. Tyrants are helping me get free, as I learn how to stop giving them any power in my life. I need them at this stage in my development.

You and your learning partner or partners should identify the petty tyrants in your lives, get to understand how they prick your self-importance and how you respond to them with self-pity and victim stories. Holding certain people in your consciousness as petty tyrants requires a bad explanation of what is going on. Your victim story is the bad explanation.

Deconstruct the victim story and embrace these people by inviting them into your examination. Once you see who they are, people like us who are going to die, and see how you have given them immense power to bring you down by assuming they are doing something to you, your petty tyrants will all disappear as realities in your own psyche. Remember, even if you have a real bad person in your life, that person is your invention and cannot control how you feel, think or behave, if you take creative control of your emotions, thinking and behavior.

People who tyrannize other people are people who feel victimized themselves. Full of self-pity, they are angry men and women who think that someone has done or is doing something to them. Consciously or unconsciously, tyrants want others to suffer in payment for their suffering. Poised, we will creatively ward off their toxic interactions with us, but we will not blame them for our own self-pity. We can only embrace them for the valuable role they play in our learning, however unconscious they are about their gift to us.

Your gratitude will soar when you can see clearly the difference between the self-pitying tyrant's shrunken life and your life of sustained poise. How fortunate for you, and how unfortunate for the petty tyrant, trapped in a bad explanation of life, a bad explanation that you are familiar with because you have abandoned it for a much better explanation.

A milestone in sustaining poise is the realization that you no longer have even one petty tyrant in your life, and no new ones are showing up. You have successfully relegated self-pity to the harmless place in the background of your moment-to-moment awareness.

POISED MOST OF THE TIME

As we master a sustained poise, we notice how much energy is required to maintain our bad explanations that still defend self-pity, and we become less and less willing to waste our energy creating victim stories and defending them.

Most of the time, at this stage, we are able to welcome life flowing in, no matter what is happening. Day after day, good hours pile up one after the other. Almost all of the time, we are present in each wonderful moment. We feel connected to our fellow human beings and to the earth which sustains us.

We don't complain anymore, and we receive life's abundance with humble gratitude. Our creativity rises out of our poise, solving every problem and making the most of every opportunity. Our hearts are light. Even in the face of challenges, we know that life will prevail. On a path of love, we acquiesce.

But even after much work and many successes, we may be chagrined to find that we can still lose our poise in subtle ways, that we still give energy to remnants of our self-pity.

If you have reached this level of consciousness, be of good heart. You are getting close to withdrawing all energy from self-pity. We can continue to reveal these vulnerabilities to our learning partners and help each other become even more alert for still unresolved issues that need our attention and commitment. We're in the home stretch and victory is near, so we want to finish the job and fly free.

Chances are that the victimhood remaining is only the shadow of the self-pity we have already identified and abandoned. There's a bit more, a final resistant strain that needs to be cleaned up.

Clean it up, even if life is pretty wonderful most of the time and better than it has ever been. Finish.

5

No More Energy
for the Victim

CHANGING PERSONAL RELATIONSHIPS

You will naturally have new challenges as you master greater poise. You have vanquished the victim within, no longer giving it any energy in your life. Your thinking and behavior have changed, so your relationships will change.

People close to you may feel that you are easier to be around these days, more peaceful, but—absorbed in their own challenges—they may not recognize the transformation you have made unless you have told them about it explicitly and with some thoroughness. You have made a transformation, but others may continue to relate to you as if you are still the person they have been familiar with for some time.

You will notice that some of the people closest to you are still operating out of the same assumptions that used to be your assumptions. You notice that you don't enjoy some of the usual banter with friends, family or co-workers, especially the highly patterned exchanges of complaints, ego fortifying, and cynicism.

Some of the people in your life leave you depleted because they ask you to give energy to their victimhood. Most people have not addressed very seriously their self-pity, so they are operating out of bad explanations. They want you to give your energy and support to these bad explanations. They want rescuing from whatever petty tyrants they have created.

You may have tried already to withdraw your energy from their victim stories by offering your perspective – offering better explanations for their suffering. You may have talked about the advantages of sustaining poise. Chances are that your better explanations have not been welcomed but instead rejected as unrealistic and uncaring: "Can't you understand what I'm going through? Don't you care about me?"

You may need to withdraw your energy from these relationships altogether in order to have the energy you need to fuel your own development. When you see that none of your kind coaching is being accepted, that you are being resented by your friends or family members because you don't agree with their victim story, you face a conundrum – continue providing energy to their self-pity or pull away.

We care about these people and our relationships with them, so withdrawing our energy from them is not easy. If you find yourself unable to withdraw support for their victim stories, it could mean that your own self-pity resonates with theirs.

You are still energizing your own victimhood. In other words, you still have work to do.

Or it might be that you are reluctant to withdraw energy from their victimhood because of a stubborn moral perspective that directs you never to give up on someone, even if there is no evidence that the person wants to learn anything new or wants to make any changes at all. So, if you continue to give energy to this person who is resisting all invitations for a learning dialogue, you will have to assume that you have unlimited energy to waste, a bad explanation for what is going on.

An alternative to pouring energy into a resistant situation is to offer support and dialogue later if there is a change of mind, making it clear, however, that you won't be providing any more energy for the victim story.

You are not abandoning this person but are simply withdrawing your energy from victimhood as a way of releasing yourself from a diminished life. You are refusing to support a bad explanation – one that is not only a lie, but which is injuring the person who creates it by blocking growth and development.

Your decision to change the nature of your relationship is an expression of your clarity and love.

Your decision to pull away from a loved one's self-pity is a powerful indication that you have cut off all energy from your own self-pity.

Your loved one will react to your decision to withdraw support and energy with more self-pity, and you may well be cast in the role of petty tyrant yourself as this transition in your relationship unfolds.

What can you do but sustain your poise throughout this transition? You have made a transformational change so, of course, your relationships must change. Letting go of relationships that are stuck, in spite of your best efforts, will make way for the relationships you need at the next stage of your development.

You need your energy for emergence.

NO MORE ENERGY FOR COLLECTIVE VICTIMHOOD

As we sustain poise, it is not only individuals locked in victimhood who deplete our energy, but societal victimhood as well.

Connected continuously to the communal narrative, as we are now in the electronic era, we realize that self-pity and victimhood, followed by victim story after victim story, are the major themes of the human narrative at this point in our evolution.

Much of our communal dialogue is angry, irritated, and impatient, a sure indicator of self-pity and victimhood. In the national dialogue, the political parties, the government, the lobbyists, the wealthy, the poor, the unions, the insurance companies – to name some of our favorites – become our petty tyrants, the targets of our projections.

At the click of a switch, we also hear and see fellow human beings doing inspiring things, joyfully giving their love in service and innovation, developing better and better explanations in every arena of human life. Millions of people – perhaps tens or hundreds of millions of people – all over the Earth are living their lives in a poised consciousness – present, connected, grateful, creative, and lighthearted. Some of these people are in close proximity in our everyday world, inspiring us wherever we have the good fortune to join them in action or observe them close-up.

Still, the din of angry victimhood is dominant much of the time, and we find our energy depleted by it. Even though we find the angry communal victim stories of some leaders and their followers onerous and false, we may tune in to them, addicted to the dominating power of highly skilled ideologues, who want us to join their cause by agreeing with their bad explanation of what is happening.

We may or may not be personally engaged with the work of changing society, but our own dialogue with friends, colleagues and acquaintances about our communal issues may re-create the victim stories.

In opposition to the aggrieved victim story of a political leader or party, for instance, we may unconsciously argue our opposition with the same tones of grievance. In resistance to the false victim story, we end up telling another victim story, replete with us good guys as the victims of the tyrants on the other side of the argument.

These communal victim exchanges are the perfect example of life in the eddy, all of us going round and round, as if we are on the move, but never going anywhere.

OUR CHANGING RELATIONSHIP WITH THE HUMAN RACE

To the extent that we find ourselves perpetuating the communal victim stories, we are giving energy to victimhood. We are still hooked, however subtly, to our own self-pity. We are not sustaining our poise.

We may argue that we are lending a thoughtful, well-informed, enlightened voice to the communal dialogue. We might acknowledge that we are not doing all that much good insofar as achieving change is concerned, but we are taking a principled stance for good citizenship. But if we hear ourselves still creating victim stories, still acting aggrieved, still projecting our displeasure onto others, still playing the righteously angry critic or rescuer, still separating ourselves from others, we are not sustaining poise.

A friend suggests that I am ignoring what he calls "righteous indignation," a virtuous anger that advocates for the weak against the powerful. Here is a sophisticated victim story from a sophisticated rescuer. No, there is no such thing as virtuous anger. Anger, carried beyond the first moment we feel it, always emanates out of self-pity, creating a victim story and all of the errors in perception that come with a very bad explanation.

So-called righteous indignation is simply a cover-up of the ego's need to display its virtue. If we find ourselves defending virtuous anger, we know we still have work to do exposing our own self-pity, which continues to resonate with the suffering of the human race. We may advocate and take on tough battles, of course, but we will control our folly as we pursue our life calling, and we will sustain our poise.

So what happens if we withdraw our energy from the communal victim story, as we withdrew it from our personal relationships?

There are some things we don't have to do. We don't have to stop being highly informed citizens. We don't have to stop engaging in social and political processes. We don't have to stop caring about the well-being of other people. We don't have to stop talking and planning with others. We don't have to become cynical and judgmental. We don't have to withdraw our love.

We do have to control our folly by refusing to provide energy to the communal victim story. Our artistic contribution to any dialogue about communal issues will be an attempt to derail the victim stories as they emerge, revealing them as the bad explanations that they are and offering some better explanations for consideration and testing.

Our explanations won't star any victims in a melodrama of victimhood. They won't honor any anger. Our good explanations will argue that a human being is not a leaf at the mercy of the wind, but a magical creature that can create better and better explanations into infinity. We can make the case for

living in the now, for being connected, for a humble gratitude, for approaching the problems of the human race with
optimism and creativity and, finally, for enjoying this life
with the wisdom of the light heart.

If the people we talk to regularly find us contrary or naïve, if
they cannot contribute to a poised dialogue but instead keep
slipping back into the victim explanation, we can artfully
continue to guide the conversation. Or we can find some
other people to talk to.

Either way, we consciously commit to sustaining our poise
by refusing any energy for the established victim explanation of the moment. Loving life, we steer ourselves out of
the eddy and move off into the flow, even if few are ready to
go with us right now.

STATIC IN OUR LEARNING RELATIONSHIPS

As we stop giving energy to people's self-pity and victim stories, we will likely appreciate even more our life-embracing
partners who have helped us master sustained poise. These
are our most intimate and rewarding relationships. These
partners have been friends and trusted confidantes. We have
made breakthroughs together as fellow seekers.

But sometimes these invaluable learning relationships falter
or break apart to some extent, even though they have been
the dynamic center of our life, the source of support, feedback and love as we reduced our self-pity and victimhood
and gained a new threshold of sustained poise.

If you have relied mostly on one key person, a spouse or some other committed partner, you have been enjoying a life-giving dialogue that has produced immense benefit. Thanks to the learning you have done with your loved one or with your loving partners, you are sustaining your poise most of the time, and life is richer, more exciting and wondrous than it has ever been. Together, you have been pioneering on the frontiers of human emergence. Two people with the same commitment, working together, are a dynamic energy. You have been probing deeply held explanations of life that are flawed.

But now, one of you seems to be backing off, apparently less interested in this rigorous process, still holding remnants of self-pity and still telling subtle victim stories. Whatever has happened to end the learning process prematurely, one partner is less committed than before, leaving the other partner in some consternation.

If your partner no longer seeks your feedback about self-pity, victim stories and loss of poise and, in fact, becomes defensive when you offer your observations and support, you face a dilemma. You have faith in your partner and hate to accept this lapse in commitment. You want to continue the dialogue. Clearly, however, your partner has not fully embedded the new awareness about self-pity, victim stories and sustaining poise and seems to be regressing. When you press the issue or even inquire about what your partner is thinking, you may find yourself becoming the petty tyrant in your partner's victim story.

Now what?

First, if we are to sustain poise, our new mantra must be: no more energy for the victim.

This injunction now unexpectedly applies to your partner. You have to withhold your energy from your partner's victim story – especially when you have been thrust into the role of persecutor. As with other people who insist on bad explanations for their challenges, you can offer a better explanation – even though you and your partner have probed these issues before.

You can explain to your partner how valuable your learning relationship has been to you, how much you have enjoyed your partnership, and how much you hope it will continue. If your partner continues to hold fast to the victim explanation, all you can do is to offer your availability if there is a change of mind.

You may see your partner return to the dialogue later. You may have to move on to other learning relationships, sustaining your poise, of course, as you go.

One thing for sure: We meet the people we need at every stage of development.

Sustaining your poise every day, you will have poised friends. Your closest relationships will be the best relationships you have ever enjoyed. As usual, all will be provided.

6

Breaking Through: A Love Story

The following example highlights how you can play your role as a learning partner to someone learning to sustain poise.

Judy is a good friend of mine who recently lost her poise over an incident in Kenya, where she has been serving a Quaker mission. She invited me to join her as her learning partner to investigate what she calls "a meltdown." She wanted to discover why she has been so anguished over what happened.

My purpose here is to show how the learning relationship works as we confront issues of lost poise with each other. I have reported the course of our dialogue over a period of weeks, pretty much the way it happened.

Judy is the ideal learning partner because – even though she finds this process as challenging as anyone else – she is a fearless seeker who does not shy away from her own learning, no matter how painful it might be. She also has a great sense of humor, a huge asset in this process.

At the end of the story, I provide tips for things to notice about your role as learning partner.

LEARNING TOGETHER TO SUSTAIN POISE

Judy is a 67 year-old white woman, a Quaker who embodies her church's main tenet that God calls each of us to service. She has always been a committed and skilled advocate for people society often holds at arm's length – the poor, the mentally ill and racial minorities.

Judy and her former husband, an African American man, raised five children in a 30-year marriage.

For the past five years, Judy has taken a leave of absence each year from her work with the chronically mental ill to be a Quaker volunteer in Kenya, working as a nurse first in an urban ghetto health clinic and more recently in a remote rural hospital. She raises her own money for her expenses for 12-week stints each year. Here is the initial victim story Judy told me about how she experienced a colossal loss of poise:

> As one of only three white women in my rural Kenyan community, I am constantly besieged by strangers on the road asking for money. Kenyans in this region live in deep poverty, but I am not rich enough to give

money to every stranger who asks, even though I have great empathy for the people here. I have given money many times, however, to acquaintances and neighbors who were in need. I also have loaned money to people I work with and have been paid back most of the time.

On my last trip I was asked for substantial loans by my driver, a man I have hired to drive me for five years, and a teacher I engaged to teach me Swahili. In both cases, I was careful to negotiate a repayment plan that would pay me the money back before I returned to the United States. My driver had already worked off one loan I gave him. The language teacher had been a reliable and competent tutor, for which I paid him well, maybe too much, each session. I trusted both men and felt assured of repayment.

Neither man paid me back, and I was dumbfounded and angry. How did I miss the obvious? I didn't see it coming. It's part of the Kenyan culture, I think now, to be unable to fulfill what you promise to do. The teacher did not pay on the day he had promised. When I called him to pursue repayment, he said he would pay me the next day. He didn't show up. Two days before I was to return home, I called again and he told me his wife would come by with the money, but she never showed up. I think his actions were intentional.

My driver didn't pay on the promised date either. He apologized to me on my last day in Kenya when he picked me up to take me to the airport but said he could not repay. I have known him and his family for five years, so I felt profoundly disappointed and angry. When he told me that he didn't have the money to pay me back, I could have cried. I felt betrayed by both of them. I feel as a white American woman, I am marked.

On the flight home I was disturbed. I obsessed about what had just happened. Then I got the shingles as soon as I got home. Shingles is caused by stress and for a month I had to treat the painful, oozing sores on my body. My partner was sympathetic, but he was angry with me for being naïve enough to lend these two men so much money. I've told my family and friends what happened to me, and they have all been supportive and sympathetic.

That was two months ago. I'm not obsessing about these two men so much now, although I must admit that I cannot forgive them.

> I have decided to change my approach when I
> return to Kenya for my service next year. First,
> I'm going to shorten my service from twelve to
> six weeks. Also, I will be much more on guard
> when people want money from me. I certainly
> will not be engaging the teacher again, and
> as things stand now, I will not be rehiring my
> driver again either. I will be, no doubt, less
> generous in future visits and less likely to be
> taken advantage of. I feel some despair about
> Kenya because of what happened. I'm pulling
> back a bit; my guard is up.

After she returned to the United States, Judy realized that this incident was significant. She had the shingles. She was obsessing about the betrayals. She told the story above – her explanation – to family and friends, who gave her agreement and support, but she felt stuck and unable to move on.

When she shared the story with me, I identified it as a victim story, a bad explanation for what had happened. I pointed out that her continuing anger was the tip-off to her self-pity. She agreed that she had been feeling sorry for herself and agreed that she had cooked up a victim story. She tried to create an explanation about Kenyan society as the culprit, but that story was an attempt to deflect her feelings of personal betrayal. She was still in the victim mode.

WHAT'S BEING REJECTED?
I asked her to list the things she was rejecting in this situation. What's disturbing you? Who can't you forgive? What

is triggering your anger and anguish? What would you like to eliminate from life right now? She came up with the following:

- I reject the idea that it's OK to promise to pay back a loan and then default on your promises.
- I reject the idea that promises made to rich white Americans don't have to be honored because they don't have to live in poverty and danger, so they will be OK if they don't get paid back.
- I reject the hypocrisy of Kenyans who claim to be Christians but fail to live up to the teachings of Christ.

When we reject things in life, we are likely to develop victim stories to explain how life should be. And when we're stuck in the bad explanation – the victim story – we are usually viewing the situation through a too-small frame.

In this case, Judy's frame was her relationship with two African men she trusted with a loan but who later betrayed her trust.

In our dialogue, Judy and I moved to the larger frame of her life purpose. She volunteered that her life purpose is advocacy. Having known her for decades, I was able to point out that her advocacy involved crossing boundaries that others are reluctant to cross. I remembered that she has always created loving, trusting relationships with people marginalized by poverty, criminal behavior, severe mental illness, and racial minority status. For all of us privileged to know her,

Judy is a model of love and acceptance, of loving others as herself. Judy is a boundary crosser in the realms of love.

Most of her friends, I pointed out, see her work in Kenya as qualification for sainthood. It is a country with great turmoil. It is sometimes violent and dangerous. In Judy's rural Kenyan community, the water is often not running. Electricity is unpredictable. There's malaria. There is the constant discomfort of seeing people in desperate need everywhere you look. Children brought in to the hospital from the bush villages are often too sick to be healed. This is love's hard duty, and Judy has faithfully carried out her spirit's duty. Many Kenyans have told Judy how much she has helped and how much she is appreciated.

So, now this. In situations where our victim stories obscure the truth, our learning partners may be able to discern what is hidden. Because Judy said she couldn't see anything beyond her victim story, I suggested for Judy's consideration what I believe is a better explanation for what happened. As her learning partner, here was my first attempt at a good explanation:

> In my life of service, I practice loving others as myself. To do that, I must cross boundaries to establish loving relationships with people other people might avoid or even hate. I have been richly rewarded with love coming back to me from so many people I have served. I have taken into my embrace the poorest

of the poor, the mentally disabled and those marginalized because of their race.

In mostly white Iowa where I live, I crossed the racial boundary many decades ago to marry a black man, and we raised our children – white and black together. In recent years, I have crossed several boundaries to serve in Kenya as a nurse – stiff boundaries of race, geography and wealth. People who have few advantages have accepted me there, by and large, and I have formed loving relationships with the people we serve at the hospital and with my black colleagues, even though it is not always easy.

On my last visit, I loaned quite a lot of money to two Kenyans I knew and trusted. Neither man has much money, but both promised to pay me back in full before I returned to the states. Neither man paid me, and I left Kenya deeply disappointed and angry. In spite of the over-all positive experience I had over the past 12 weeks in Kenya, I obsessed about this betrayal all the way home on the plane, and then when I got home, I immediately got the shingles. My mind was in distress, and my body was pain-fully aflame with the evidence of it.

For weeks I told my partner, friends and fam-ily and other loved ones a victim story about how I had been betrayed, how I was cutting down on my commitment to my Kenya mission, how I had made a mistake in judgment, how hopeless Kenyan culture is, and how I wouldn't be loaning money to anyone when I return next year. I also said I wasn't able to forgive those two men and that I would not be likely to have anything to do with them in the future. Everyone gave me sympathy and support, and the issue gradually has lost steam but was not resolved.

My initial victim story was false, a distortion, a lie. What really happened was that I forgot my mission – crossing boundaries to love the unloved. Instead, I wanted reciprocity for my gifts of love to the two men I loaned money to. I gave them love, yes, but only as long as I thought I would be paid back. When I wasn't paid back, I no longer had access to my love, as evidenced by my lost poise. Self-pity took over, and I invented a righteous victim story to highlight the plight of the loving woman who has been wronged.

Yes, I am a loving woman but have learned in this incident that I can lose access to my love when it is not reciprocated. My love will be complete when I can give it without expectation of return. In this case, my love had conditions. Actually, unconditional love is my state of consciousness most of the time, so I can close this gap in my awareness without too much trouble. I forgive my two Kenyan associates and bring them back into my love's embrace. Nobody is doing anything to anybody, let alone to a woman of service like me.

When I return to Kenya, I will not forget again what I'm doing there: crossing boundaries to love, nurture and heal. Maybe I'll make loans to people in need again; maybe not. But if I do, I will know in advance that the loan is a gift, and if I'm paid back, I'll know it's because the love I give is always returned in some way.

BARRICADED BEHIND BAD EXPLANATIONS

It is not easy to see how we are barricaded behind our bad explanations. Judy was intrigued by my explanation, but she continued to see the explanation of her suffering outside herself, wondering again if Kenya's culture is the ultimate cause.

It's universally difficult for us to see our problems as projections of our own incomplete consciousness. Learning partners need to keep probing beyond the bad explanation, which may get repeatedly defended as the dialogue proceeds.

So I took another tack with the question, "I'm assuming that you are creating every aspect, detail and outcome of your life. Why did you create this situation?"

In answer, Judy wondered if she loaned the two men money to "look good," to "feel good." She suggested that her ego created this situation, that her self-image is enhanced when she helps people who are in need. She said she loans money to her mentally ill clients in the states frequently.

Then she remembered to say that the driver had been extremely nervous when he asked for the loan and also that he had sent her an e-mail a couple of days ago apologizing again for not repaying.

I suggested that the world we describe is probably a projection of ourselves and wondered if the two men didn't represent some aspect of herself – her lack of integrity to her commitments, for instance. Is there part of you, I asked, that is poor of spirit, weak and seemingly hapless? Wouldn't your pullback in commitment in your mission from twelve weeks to six weeks be significant, along with your decision to give less money in the future?

I suggested that our troubles frequently arise in the center of our strengths. I observed that Judy is full of love and generosity, and that everybody close to her knows her as an exemplar of integrity. This anguish, I suggested, is your potential screaming at you to pay some attention to an internal inconsistency – some flaw in your integrity in relationships. What potential is opened up in this situation? Judy couldn't come up with much in the moment.

I tried yet another tack. Why did she object so dramatically to not being paid back? I suggested that these two men made promises but ultimately took more than they gave. I wondered if Judy is so disturbed because she herself takes more than she gives. I pointed out that each trip to Kenya is partially paid for by over one hundred of her friends, who contribute money each year. You have recruited an army of support, I said, and you are the star of this mission drama, inviting lots of attention, support, and love for yourself.

She laughed and agreed – that she likes all the attention she gets over her Kenya service.

I asked her what she gets out of her Kenya service. She said she gets several benefits:

- Warm winters.
- People liking and appreciating me.
- Lots of warmth and love.
- Feeling needed.

She added that she does not get the same benefits in her job at home with the chronically mentally ill. Their needs are overwhelming and require most of the energy in their relationship. She has to give a lot and must find her rewards in knowing that she is reducing the suffering of others. In the Kenya mission, however, she gets lots of attention and appreciation.

SEARCHING FOR THE BEST EXPLANATION

I remembered that when we lose our poise we always lose access to our love and give less than we get from life.

Not poised, we stand resisting life with our arms folded stubbornly over our hearts.

Is it possible, I asked, circling back to the possibility that I had raised earlier, even though you are very generous, that you take more than you give in your Africa mission?

"Oh, boy," she responded, not liking this possibility.

How are you doing with Gene (her partner) these days, I asked? Do you take more than you give?

Judy said that she has been worrying about that very problem lately. She sees that Gene gives her more than he gets from her in their relationship. She has been wondering if she doesn't give too much attention to her work and not enough attention to his potential.

She has contemplated correcting this imbalance by working less and devoting much more time and energy to his interests, service, and potential. She's been worried about getting more than she gives with Gene, a loved one she holds in high regard for his unending generosity and humble service to others, she said.

I asked, "Isn't this where your potential lies? Your recent anguish about not being paid back – your victim story – was a wake-up about a deeper issue that may play out repeatedly in your life."

After several days of reflection, Judy wrote down another version of the story – what she considered now to be a better explanation of her lost poise. She concludes her revised story by saying:

> Describing my behavior is painful, but I know I need to work on it. I need to change. Here it is: I take more than I give in Kenya. I know what this dynamic feels like because I've been on the giving end in situations at work or in personal relationships where I give way more than I get. With Micah and James, I took more than I gave. Yes, I paid them for their work, but my relationship with them was essential to my daily well being in Kenya. They did not pay back the loans, a hard lesson to me about who owed what to whom. I owed Kenya for my starring role as a missionary and all the gratitude, support and praise I received in that role. Overall, I owed a debt to Kenya and all the people I met there. Sure, two of those people lied, but I had been warned and did not listen.

> OK. So now I know what my behavior was. Now how do I work on preventing it from happening over and over again so that I am able to retain my poise?

Judy has begun to change her Kenya story as a result of our dialogue and my suggestions. She now puts most of the responsibility on herself. She is beginning to see that she gets more out of her Kenya mission than she gives and that perhaps she wasn't so generous after all. Still, she mentions that she had been warned about lending money to Kenyans, suggesting that she still thinks part of her anguish was caused by them, not herself.

In our next set of conversations, totaling several hours, Judy revealed that her anguish after she left Kenya was even worse than she had initially reported. After much give and take, here is her final explanation of why she lost her poise and was unable to retrieve it until we examined the cause:

JUDY'S GOOD EXPLANATION

On the plane trip home I was very angry and upset. I was in pain emotionally and physically. I couldn't sleep. I was uncomfortable and my body began to hurt. I was berating myself for the loans and wondered how I would tell Gene when I got home.

Within three days of my getting home to Des Moines, I was so ill I wanted to die, in spite of the anti-viral meds and the pain meds I was taking for the shingles. I was in excruciating pain, barely conscious, actually ready for death.

During my month of illness, I continued to be obsessed about the betrayal, about not being paid back, and I continued to tell my story to get sympathy. Now I realize that part of my anguish was due to a growing worry that my entire mission in Kenya was folly. I had accumulated heavy evidence over five years of volunteer work there that the Quaker hospital where I volunteered was badly managed. There was evidence of executive corruption. The CEO, a Kenyan manager, may have been skimming funds. The local Kenyan board of directors was incompetent and unable to hold management accountable. The Quaker church sponsors in the United States had not intervened adequately, even though I and others on the ground in Kenya had informed them about possible corruption.

I had solicited all my friends and family for support based on a different story about the mission – that this was a worthy and noble mission doing lots of good, with me the star, noble Judy doing heroic and beneficial work in a troubled land.

My story was collapsing fast: I have been doing some good work in Kenya, but I have to admit now that my work really hasn't done anything to change the fundamental problems of the hospital – its corruption, lack of accountability to the board, and the irresponsibility and denial of the Quaker sponsors in the United States.

I've just been piddling in Kenya for five years – at least in the context of the real problems that need addressing if better health care is to be developed for the Kenyans who depend on the hospital as their only hope. I have been worried about these realities for some time, but now it all comes together with sharp clarity.

What collapsed was my delusion that I can save people, that I can save the hospital, that I can save those two men I loaned money to. This delusion was my ego's construct, with me as the star, deserving of lots of people's attention, love, financial support, and interest. To create and sustain this delusion, I'm saying, in effect, "Look at me, everybody! I'm special. I'm interesting. I'm talented. I'm unique. Notice that I'm fully alive! Give me your energy!"

All of this is dead now; I've used it all up. The grandiosity has collapsed. I'm living in the real world now and will no longer be telling the heroic Judy story to get support from my family and friends.

The self-importance I bolstered with my Kenya mission got deflated and the underlying self-pity got exposed. My ego construct about noble Judy was already coming apart; I had worried for some time about the real story at the hospital and the real story about the effectiveness of my work there.

The final blow was not getting paid back – in other words, the real value of my work was indicated by not getting paid. I was already getting more than I received in Kenya. I got lots of personal goodies for years from this service but didn't actually contribute very much of permanent value. To some extent, I feel I was a bit of a fraud. When the delusion was shattered, I came apart for a while. Shingles? Maybe I had to shed my old skin.

I'm better off now, my potential available to me in a way that has been closed off by my delusions of grandeur. I'm grounded again, and I'm happy again – back to my usual joyful self. I'll let the two men know that all is forgiven, including the debts. I'll return to Kenya one last time for closure. I will soon attend the Quaker's annual conference where I will have an opportunity to advise U.S. church leaders of the need to train and develop the local hospital board as the only way to bring needed accountability and leadership to the hospital's mission.

In the future, I am going to invest in Gene's potential by following him into international missions of his choice. I'm on a path of love, and I'll be more effective with this lesson. I'll be poised.

Judy has made a breakthrough and now speaks with a powerfully poised voice. The self-pity is gone. The victim story
is gone. She isn't obsessing, and she isn't looking for sympathy or rescuing. She takes full responsibility for her entire
experience in Kenya, and reports with great insight her ques-
tionable motives, the real value of her service, and the nature
of her relationship with the two men. She has acknowledged
how the Kenya service gave her more than she gave to it.

Her love is flowing again. She easily forgives. She is happy.
Still investing in her real mission in Kenya, she commits her
leadership to a strategy that might have significant impact.
She sees her relationship with Gene with a new clarity,
and she makes a new, loving commitment to him and his
potential.

The potential Judy is moving into is the potential we arrive
at with successful inquiries into self-pity, victim stories, and
lost poise. It's the potential to access our full love.

As a learning partner in the inquiry, you will know if you're
getting somewhere if you and your learning partner realize
that expanding love is the answer. This is always the final
destination in a search for the foundations of poise.

TIPS FOR HELPING YOUR LEARNING PARTNER MAKE A BREAKTHROUGH

1. Don't buy the victim story. Your learning partner will
   probably make a strong case for it and won't give it
   up easily. You, as a nice person, may feel uncomfortable arguing that the victim story is a distortion, a

bad explanation, a lie. But it is, and you must make that argument, if your learning partner genuinely invites your dialogue. Your main gift to your learning partner, as a matter of fact, is to challenge the victim story. Even if you don't have much insight about a better explanation immediately, you can do much to help by deconstructing the victim story. Keep insisting that your partner is creating his life – every bit of it, even if he doesn't see that reality right now. The most respect you can give him is to give him credit for the life he is creating. Any other response from you is enabling or condescension. If you buy the victim story, you're both lost.

2. Suggest possible explanations to replace the victim story but avoid advice. As learning partners, we are creative seekers, peering into the unknown with our partner. We don't have the answer, so we can't give advice. Advice doesn't help anyway. It only derails the dialogue as it serves our own ego. For example, what about my idea that Judy forgive the loans; isn't that advice? No, it's a suggestion for consideration and maybe not the right suggestion. Judy might have objected to forgiving the loans on the grounds that she does not want to enable these two men, who need to learn to keep their commitments. Or maybe she needs the money. Either way, I'm not attached to what she decides. In fact, I want her to decide for herself. I'm priming the pump with my suggestions, and she will take it from there. I avoid saying, "You should." That's advice.

3. In the dialogue, stay focused on the anguish, the suffering, and what is being rejected. Your learning partner may want to shy away from the disturbance, but you can help by staying with it until you see what it disguises. The disturbance is our potential hollering at us, and we need to figure out what it is calling our attention to. Your partner probably will be willing to talk about the disturbance, but deflect the discomfort with the victim story explanation. We need to keep asking, "What within *you* is disturbed?" You may have to come back to the discomfort over and over. This introspection is tough.

4. Encourage your partner to retell the story as if he is creating everything in the story. Judy had a hard time saying, "I loaned money that was not repaid. Then I decided to be angry and be upset. Then I decided to get shingles to wake myself up to what was going on. Then I told and retold my victim story to loved ones because I knew they would give me comfort and never challenge my version of what happened. Then I obsessed about these two men, convincing myself that they are very imperfect beings. Then I decided to cut back on my commitment to Kenya to punish them for what they did to me." If your partner can't retell the story in this way, do it for him, so he can become familiar with this strategy and its potential to reveal the truth. Telling our victim stories in this way creates some very funny versions of what we're up to, and we can laugh together about how absurd we are capable of being. So be light and loving as

you retell the story as if your partner had been fully conscious, doing all this crazy stuff on purpose.

5. As you offer better explanations for your partner's consideration, remember that this problem may lie right in the center of your partner's strengths. That fact allows you to discuss what your partner is missing in a larger, positive frame. Notice that the first explanation I offered Judy to replace her victim story recognizes and accentuates her strengths of love, integrity and service. In other words, I make sure to emphasize that her anger and lack of forgiveness with the two men is not characteristic of her; it's a rare contradiction in a loving and generous life. I give her credit for creating her life and assume that she in inviting this introspection because she is conscientious. In my suggested explanation, I present Judy in all of her characteristic generosity.

Most people, in my experience, underestimate how difficult real learning is. As learning partners, we have a delicate role. We have to contest the self-pity and victim stories without blinking, and, at the same time, we have to remind our learning partner about the many strengths he brings to this challenge.

Anybody ready for this rigorous level of learning brings a pretty mature consciousness so you will have plenty of evidence to draw on as you create a positive framework for this particular problem. If you focus only on the mistakes your partner is making with this particular situation and don't constantly maintain the positive framework, your partner will not feel supported enough to stay with the process. Even the strongest people find this work daunting, so give honest feedback with lots of love and support.

6. Listen deeply. This is obvious, of course. But the listening required in a learning dialogue like this one requires several things of us. First, we must see potential in our partner and must be excited to pursue that potential. Shining your light into her dark corners is love in action. Our partner must see that we have faith that she can learn something valuable here that will expand her life. You have a stake here; your relationship is strengthened if new consciousness is achieved. Her potential becomes your potential.

Second, we may know our partner quite well, as I knew Judy very well when we began our dialogue about the Kenya trouble, but I didn't know enough and never will. I have to listen. In this case, I learned some new things as our dialogue progressed: I heard for the first time the personal benefits she gets out of her mission, and I saw that her mission gives her something her work in the United States does not. I didn't know how much she likes all the attention she gets as she enlists us all to support her mission. I had not known about her growing disillusionment with her Kenya mission. I didn't know she has been worried about not giving enough to Gene. This and much more of what I heard helped me suggest what a good explanation might look like.

Finally, deep listening will make a dialogue of discovery possible. Fritz Perls observed that most people cannot have a true conversation because they have either no ears and can only talk, or they have no voice and can only listen. The learning dialogue requires that we both talk and listen. When we do, we put into motion an exciting creative process fueled by two brains, four ears and four eyes, two sets of life experiences.

When we listen deeply, we make discoveries together, connect more dots together, and see more possibilities than we saw without each other. We are warrior travelers, looking, looking, breathlessly.

7. Keep reminding yourself and your learning partner throughout your dialogue that you are moving toward potential. We're moving toward an expanded awareness full of rewards. Life is going to be better, more rewarding, as we learn to sustain poise. Yes, this is difficult, but we're mining for gold in these hills of suffering. If we can learn about our self-pity and our distorted explanations, we will fly free, and there will be no need to repeat these painful lessons in the future.

8. Celebrate when breakthroughs occur. As your learning partner moves self-pity into the background and

develops a better explanation for what is happening, poise expands, and you have plenty of reason for celebration. Sustained poise is a hard-won gain deserving of acknowledgment. You are fellow students in the game of life, and you have both just created a bigger island of awareness to live on. Life is better because you see more of it than you did before, and you will both get to keep these gains from now on. You are freer than before, and the world just became a more conscious place.

7

Sustained Poise and the Survival of the Planet

We know that we are sustaining poise when we are able to spot self-pity in the moment and watch it slide obediently and harmlessly out of sight. We don't invent victim stories to explain our challenges anymore.

We don't complain about anything, ever. We are living in a new level of consciousness all day, every day. We love to be present in the now, even when challenges present themselves. We treasure our connections to other people and to this bountiful earth.

We carry an awareness each moment that we are one with the universe, a magical being in a magical reality. We feel humble about the many gifts that flow into our life every day. Not taking anything for granted, we don't let our gratitude slip away, even though we now realize that life's bounty is ours as long as we are alive.

Our disturbances call us to our potential so we don't avoid them but move toward them.

We have developed a trust in our creativity because it never fails us. We always have options, and we have become masters of improvisation.

Realizing our immense good fortune at the discoveries we have made, we know that it would be bad form to be heavy, earnest or pessimistic. Our only possible mood is joy, and our hearts are light no matter what is happening. We are living the best explanation of life, the life of sustained poise.

We have gained access to our love. We are able to call on it at any moment. If we allow it to drift off a bit because we're tired or sick or because of a difficult challenge, or because our ego pushed in demanding attention, we can make an immediate shift.

If we say no to life for a moment, we can recognize what is happening, open our hearts wide and say yes – yes, here I am, ready once again.

> Humanity is now faced with a stark choice: Evolve or die . . . If the structures of the human mind remain unchanged, we will always end up re-creating the same world, the same evils, the same dysfunction.
> Eckhart Tolle, *The New Earth: Awakening to Your Life's Purpose*

You, like everyone else, live in world of human turmoil. But you may be noticing that access to your love gives you personal power. Other people, whether they are sustaining their own poise or not, are drawn to you. You have influence wherever you are. You are free and unafraid. Your life is dynamic. You have abundant energy, so people find you interesting and alive. Your optimism and sanity are an antidote to the prevailing worries, fears, and bad explanations. Sustaining poise, you represent the best of human development.

You see and understand the human turmoil and dysfunction, which is merely the current level of consciousness of our species. Self-pity and victimhood are part of the warp and woof of our species at present and the central constraint on human potential. But the survival of the planet is enhanced by your commitment to your own awareness. As you become more conscious, the human species becomes more conscious. You are exploring on the frontiers of human emergence and bringing back tales of glory.

The human race may be caught in an evolutionary eddy for the moment, but whether that explains what is happening on Earth, you are not stuck in your life. Fully poised, you have such a profound sense of life and death that you can look at any tragedy with equanimity. You have no emotions to push down, no tears to repress – simply a sense of awe and wonder at it all.

Acquiescing to life, there is no doubt that you are drawn to a path of love in this lifetime, and you are treading that path impeccably. Poised, you are able to hear your calling, and you will be able to hear new callings as they emerge. You won't have to worry about whether you are serving others. Your love of life emanates from you as a gift every moment, no matter what you are doing.

You will never stop learning because you know that life offers endless mysteries. Tuned in, with access to your love, you know what to do with your life. You're doing it.

I think the Biblical author of this Psalm had people like you in mind:

Psalm 1

Blessed are the man and the woman
who have grown beyond their greed
and put an end to their hatred
and no longer nourish illusions.
But they delight in the way things are
and keep their hearts open, day and night.
They are like trees planted near flowing rivers,
which bear fruit when they are ready.
Their leaves will not fall or wither.
Everything they do will succeed.

Acknowledgements

I owe much of my clarity about human awareness and human behavior to the work of Carlos Castaneda. Aficionados of Castaneda's work will recognize how his perspectives and metaphors infuse this book in every chapter. For those familiar with his work, I recommend the profound but less-often read essays written toward the end of his life and a rare interview in 1997. They can be found in the following places:

"Introduction," The Original Teachings in a Deluxe 30th Anniversary Edition with a New Commentary by the Author, *The Teachings of Don Juan, A Yaqui Way of Knowledge*, Carlos Castaneda, University of California Press, 1998.

"Introduction" (and other commentary at the beginning of various chapters), *Magical Passes: The Practical Wisdom of the Shamans of Ancient Mexico*, Carlos Castaneda, Harper Collins, 1998.

"Introduction" and several essays entitled "Commentary," *The Wheel of Time: The Shamans of Ancient Mexico, Their Thoughts about Life, Death and the Universe*, Carlos Castaneda, LA Eidolona Press, 1998.

"Navigating Into the Unknown: An Interview with Carlos Castaneda," for the magazine, *Uno Mismo*, Chile and Argentina, February, 1997 by Daniel Trujillo Rivas.
Find at http://cleargreen.com/english/purpose/interviews.cfm

Mary Morris, my wife and fellow warrior traveler, has been contributing to my poise for 16 years. During the writing of this book over the past year, she has probed the deepest issues of poise with me nearly every day. She has been my intellectual interlocutor and an inspiration. She has made sure that I connect the dots. She is a sharp-eyed editor. Mary, without your love and support, this book would not have been written.

Friends and family who have read iterations of the book as it unfolded have contributed personal stories of lost poise, suggestions and encouragement. You have been my support team, and I am in your debt. Thank you, sister Barbara Feher, for our many conversations about poise and for your critiques. Thank you, Michael Geboy, for your careful reading and many thoughtful suggestions over several lunches. Thank you, Larry Wharton and Eleanor Brown, for your challenges to my assumptions: you helped me dig deeper.

Thank you, Jeff Paul, for your brilliant and light-hearted spiritual perspectives: you are one of my models of poise.

Thank you for trusting me with your intimate stories, Judy Davis, Peg Day, and Phee Sherline. I have learned much from our exchanges.

And thank you, Mary Sharp, for your professional editing. Now I know how your newspaper staff must have felt all those years having to pass your muster. They must have been challenged to improve their writing, and they must have been grateful to have you as an editor, as I am.

About the Author

Gary Stokes is a writer, researcher, leadership coach and teacher. His work has focused on strategies for charting transformational change as we evolve toward our personal and societal potential. In an age in which many of the world's human systems are trapped in an eddy, his work with local, state and national leaders has given him an intimate view of what is holding us in a static state and what will release us to move into our next level of potential.

Mr. Stokes was the founder and CEO of Move the Mountain Leadership Center, which partnered with leaders of federal and state agencies, national foundations, and advocacy organizations to redesign the nation's approach to reducing poverty. To that end, he was one of the key designers of two national dialogues on poverty.

He was also a member of the Open Society Institute's leadership development initiative to build democratic institutions in Eastern Europe.

He is the author of a book on organizational development and many articles on transformational leadership.

Mr. Stokes lives with his wife and collaborator, Mary Morris, in Prescott, Arizona.